Networks for Innovation in Sustainable Tourism

Case Studies and Cross-Case Analysis

Janne J Liburd
Jack Carlsen
Deborah Edwards
Editors

Networks for Innovation in Sustainable Tourism: Case Studies and Cross-Case Analysis
1st edition, 1st printing

Editors
Janne J Liburd, Jack Carlsen and Deborah Edwards

Cover designer
Christopher Besley, Besley Design.

ISBN: 978-0-7346-1151-2

Copyright

Disclaimer

Published by:
Tilde Publishing and Distribution
PO Box 72
Prahran VIC 3181 Australia
www.tup.net.au

Contents

About the editors

Dr Janne J Liburd is an Associate Professor and Director of the Centre for Tourism, Innovation and Culture at the University of Southern Denmark. She is a cultural anthropologist and her research interests are in the fields of sustainable tourism development and collaboration. She has published on epistemology, open innovation and Web 2.0, tourism education, quality of life, national park development, NGOs, festivals and events. Janne has conducted a number of research projects relating to competence development for tourism practitioners and tourism educators. She is the past Chair of the BEST Education Network (2005-2010) and serves on the executive committee.

Professor Jack Carlsen is Professor of Sustainable Tourism at Curtin University, Western Australia and Co-Director of the Curtin Sustainable Tourism Centre. He has an excellent research track record, which has produced more than 150 scholarly publications on various topics related to tourism planning, markets, development and evaluation. He has successfully collaborated with more than 50 colleagues in Australia and internationally and almost 90 percent of his publications have been co-authored. Professor Carlsen has strong international links with universities in Asia, Europe, and North America.

Dr Deborah Edwards is the Senior Research Fellow in Urban Tourism in the School of Leisure, Sport and Tourism, at the University of Technology, Sydney. Deborah's interests are in sustainable tourism management, urban tourism, tourism planning, volunteers in tourism attractions and the impacts of events. Deborah has been involved with the BEST Education Network for 10 years and is a member of the executive committee.

About the contributors

Dr Paulina Bohdanowicz-Godfrey has a PhD in energy technology (Royal Institute of Technology, Stockholm, Sweden, 2006) and a PhD in social science (University of Gdansk, Poland, 2005). Author and co-author of a number of publications and books, reviewer for internationally recognised journals, she currently holds a sustainability role at a major hospitality company. Her areas of interest include corporate responsibility aspects of the hospitality industry, with focus on eco-certification schemes, environmental reporting and benchmarking tools, as well as environmental education and awareness raising instruments in hospitality.

Professor Jack Carlsen is Professor of Sustainable Tourism at Curtin University, Western Australia and Co-Director of the Curtin Sustainable Tourism Centre. He has an excellent research track record, which has produced more than 150 scholarly publications on various topics related to tourism planning, markets, development and evaluation. He has successfully collaborated with more than 50 colleagues in Australia and internationally and almost 90 percent of his publications have been co-authored. Professor Carlsen has strong international links with universities in Asia, Europe, and North America.

Michael Kweku Commeh is a Research Fellow and Head of Applied Industrial Ceramic and Rural Energy and Entrepreneurships Development, at the Technology Consultancy Centre (TCC), College of Engineering at the Kwame Nkrumah University of Science and Technology (KNUST). He is involved in two disciplines-Material Science & Technology (Ceramics) and Rural Sustainable Development including Tourism and related issues. He has conducted research in sustainable Innovations Tourism and related issues, including biodiversity, rural energy, technology development and transfer.

Jiayi Du holds a Bachelors Degree of Tourism Management from Shanghai Institute of Foreign Trade and MSc in Tourism and Travel Management from New York University. She currently works as a college instructor at Shanghai Institute of Foreign Trade.

Dr Deborah Edwards is the Senior Research Fellow in Urban Tourism in the School of Leisure, Sport and Tourism, at the University of Technology, Sydney. Deborah's interests are in sustainable tourism management, urban tourism, tourism planning, volunteers in tourism attractions and the impacts of events. Deborah has been involved with the BEST Education Network for ten years and is a member of the executive committee.

Dr Paddy Forde is an Adjunct Professor at Curtin Business School in Perth, Western Australia. With a PhD in Management, Paddy has many years of industry and academic experience. Problem-based learning and case study application are an important interest of his; particularly within the international education environment.

Jane Hansen was the project leader of the initiative Experience Development in Danish Attractions (EDDA) and delivers training modules in communication, marketing and experience development. She holds a Master's degree in business and languages, and is certified in management and coaching. Ms Hansen has worked with tourism development for almost 15 years having been the Director of Development at the tourism organisation Fyntour and the regional DMO for Southern Denmark, Syddansk Turisme. She is currently Head of Department at Lillebaelt Academy of Professional Higher Education and is responsible for the service and tourism related programmes.

Anja Hergesell is a researcher and lecturer at MODUL University Vienna, and is conducting her PhD studies on environmentally friendly tourist behavior at the Vienna University of Economics and Business. Before joining MUV, she worked as a research assistant at the University of Southern Denmark. Anja holds a Master's degree in European Tourism Management from Bournemouth University, a BSc from the University of Southern Denmark and a Diplom from Hochschule Harz, Germany. She has gained international work experience in the hospitality industry and has been serving as secretary and executive committee member of the BEST Education Network. Her research interests include sustainable tourism, tourism planning and policy, and tourist behavior.

Dr Michael Hughes has a background in biology, natural resource management and tourism and recreation research, and has worked as a research fellow at Curtin University, Western Australia since 2004. He has interests in tourism and recreation policy and management, how people interact with nature, environmental interpretation, protected area management and strategic communication. Michael has more than 40 scholarly publications including journal papers, book chapters and refereed conference papers.

Dr Janne J Liburd is Associate Professor and Director of the Centre for Tourism, Innovation and Culture at the University of Southern Denmark. She is a cultural anthropologist and her research interests are in the fields of sustainable tourism development and collaboration. She has published on epistemology, open innovation and Web 2.0, tourism education, quality of life, national park development, NGOs, festivals and events. Janne has conducted a number of research projects relating to competence development for tourism practitioners and tourism educators. She is the past Chair of the BEST Education Network (2005-2010) and serves on the executive committee.

Larry Quick is a strategist with significant global experience in both the corporate and civic sectors, Larry's expertise includes corporate strategy, business planning, innovation, economic development, sustainability and resilience, urban and community planning. He has worked extensively in Australia and the USA. He is based in Melbourne, Australia and is Global Practice Leader of Resilient Futures and the Director of Strategy for Great Place Australia. Larry specialises in dealing with complex risks and opportunities that arise from the impacts and interplay of major immediate and emergent conditions such as energy re-orientation, climate change, disruptive technologies and global economic volatility.

Dr Nico Schulenkorf works as a lecturer for Sport Management at the University of Technology, Sydney (UTS). His research focuses on the social, cultural and psychological outcomes of sport and event projects, and in particular the role of sport in contributing to social development within and between disadvantaged communities. For several years, Nico has been involved in sport-for-development and health promotion programs in countries such as Sri Lanka, Israel and the Pacific Islands. For his long-term contribution to the advancement of social justice on an international level, Nico was awarded the 2008 UTS Vice Chancellor's Human Rights Award. Since 2011, Nico is Deputy Editor of the *Journal of Sport for Development*.

Dr Ginger Smith has over 15 years of experience as a professor of sustainability and tourism and senior executive in higher education administration with leading roles at major academic institutions including The George Washington University and American University in Washington, DC, New York University, and Ana G Mendez University System in San Juan, Puerto Rico. Dr Smith's degrees include a BA from Cornell University, an MA from the University of Delaware, and a PhD from the School of International Service, American University.

Foreword

In tourism, industrial espionage is usually very simple. Buy a ticket. Book a room. Order a meal. Indulge in an attraction. And at the same time, observe all details, compare with own facilities and reflect on all aspects. Secrets are not kept for long in tourism. Ideas travel as fast as the tourists do, if not faster. A married couple owning a small Bed and Breakfast (B&B), for example, always had their holidays abroad in facilities that resembled their own B&B, and they visited new ones every year. In a research interview, they describe their choice not as espionage, but rather as 'seeking inspiration', 'disturbing their own business routines' and also looking for confirmation that what they do is appropriate and up to standard. This is not necessarily innovation, but more likely simple product and service development.

This is, however, only half of the truth about innovation in tourism. Much of what is important for the genuine development of tourism takes place backstage, where tourists are not allowed. To illustrate, the CEO of a successful Norwegian coastal ferry line, the *Hurtigruten*, when asked about the secrets of the ferry's success, referred to the spectacular natural beauty along the route, the good food on board, the well-organised services, the comforts of the cabins and the challenges for staff and passengers during rough weather. All of these features are very observable, although many tourists are glad that North Atlantic storms are of the imagination. The CEO refused to lead the inquirers to the 'machine room', not disclosing knowledge about how the company reinvents its storytelling, trains the service attitudes of staff, choreographs the company's logistics and collaborates with suppliers and investors.

In many cases, sustainable tourism innovations occur in the 'machine room' of such undertakings. Changes and progress cannot be read as an open book, or discovered during the ordinary vacation. Systems monitoring the use of water, electricity, fuel and other consumables are often concealed. In such cases, how can we find proof when enterprises claim or apply certified green labeling? How can the technical side of sustainability be aligned with supporting management strategies and visionary marketing? How can businesses gain momentum in innovation processes so that they contribute to long-term profitability and sustainability? How can the organisational and legislative barriers be overcome to sustainable advantages, even by small-scale operations in a developing-world context? All these elements are far from explicit for simple observations, but rather embedded in innovative business models and networks. These machine rooms of sustainable tourism innovation require substantial research; the current volume captures important dimensions in this direction.

This book is an invitation to come backstage to the machine room in selected enterprises and organisations around the world. The examples are inspiring in a general sense, but also in their particular context. It is clearly demonstrated that the sustainability agenda is prevalent across the globe, in both developing and developed countries. Organisations and individuals who contributed to the research revealed some of their best practice in order to stimulate copying, further developments and continual improvement. Scandic Hotels, for instance, has installed a window to the machine room by simply publishing environmental innovation and documentation on a special website and on the back of the customer receipt, which guests can take home.

Clayton M Christensen – one of the leading writers of innovation – celebrates copying and the use of best practice as an essential source for sustained progression, albeit incremental. Numerous small improvements may benefit the quality, performance and, in this context, the sustainability of a product or service. The cases in this book provide us with detail about this stepwise progress. Examples include the involvement of farmers with tourism in 'Tasting Arizona', and the importance of guests as knowledge disseminators in the Brenu Beach Resort in Ghana. There is a constant plea for cases that can be fields of assessment for stakeholders in tourism, and that can be creatively scrutinised by students. It makes sense, it is efficient, and we need still more cases.

Christensen is, however, also warning against the best-practice mannerism in consulting and education. His argument is that some emerging innovations are so radical that they destruct existing concepts, knowledge bases, model collaborations and networks, and new business models are born. They bring death in the sense that enterprise cannot survive, jobs are lost and power balances maintained for ages are brought to an end. Self-evidently they are hard, if not impossible to predict, as the Ecocean case illustrates. Ecocean qualifies as a destructive innovation, as it turns upside down the understanding of both tourism and science. Such groundbreaking innovations are never stimulated from best practice, or, at least, are not commonly regarded as best practice in similar sectors or industries. In the Ecocean case, NASA was an integral part of the network: not exactly a conventional partner for tourism. As we face significant environmental challenges, there is need for what Schumpeter refers to as 'creative destruction' for tourism to become a net contributor to a sustainable future.

This book is an important beginning. It is an important research resource for reflection, replication and adaptation, and hopefully also for innovative networks for creative destruction of conventional wisdom.

Professor Anne-Mette Hjalager
Head, Danish Centre for Rural Research
University of Southern Denmark

Preface

The production of these case studies began in 2007 at the Business Enterprises for Sustainable Tourism Education Network (BEST EN) Think Tank held at Northern Arizona University, and continued with the ongoing support of BEST EN and sponsorship of the Curtin Business School. Ten original international case studies were produced and then substantially updated in 2012 for this publication. Contributions were sourced from BEST EN members and associates, who were encouraged to offer descriptions of innovation that would be of interest to an international audience. The resulting case studies could be considered as a convenience sample, that is, a sample design based on information gathered from members of a population who are conveniently accessible to the researcher (Jennings 2001). Ten international cases are included (four from the United States (US), two from Europe, and one each from Australia, Ghana, Sri Lanka and China).

The cases are based on primary and secondary research by the contributing authors and each case has been peer-reviewed prior to publication. Cross-case analysis (Patton 1990) was used to provide a research framework for comparing and contrasting the different types and contexts of innovation and to facilitate an integrated analysis of the drivers, barriers, processes and networks of innovation.

The cases have been prepared for use in research and teaching of innovation networks and sustainable tourism development. The analysis and case notes are both designed to facilitate discussion and further investigation of networks for innovation, not only in tourism, but in other economic sectors as well.

Janne Liburd, Jack Carlsen and Deborah Edwards
Editors

References

Jennings, G 2001, *Tourism Research*, Wiley, Australia.

Patton, MQ 1990, *Qualitative Evaluation and Research Methods*, Sage Publications, California.

Chapter 1

Introduction to networks for innovation in sustainable tourism

JANNE J LIBURD AND JACK CARLSEN

INTRODUCTION

Networks of innovation are the key to responding to the challenges for tourism organisations and destinations making the transformation to sustainability. This book assembles ten case studies of large and small enterprises from destinations in developed and developing nations that are pursuing networks of innovation to enhance the sustainability of their operations and destinations. Innovation has previously been considered as outcomes-based phenomena, or producing new products, managerial processes, marketing methods or organisational structures (Hjalager 2010). Likewise, sustainability has also been perceived as a desired state or outcome that can be achieved if a set of prescriptive steps are followed (Commonwealth of Australia 2004) or if negative ecological and social impacts minimised (Candara & Channdra 2004). *Networks for Innovation in Sustainable Tourism* takes the view that sustainability must be seen as a dynamic process of change, rather than a static goal to be achieved, and therefore must be tackled with ever-evolving, flexible strategies.

Innovation for sustainable tourism is almost always supported by networks of organisations and individuals that drive the innovation process, overcoming barriers along the way and expanding the network as the innovation is implemented. Invariably, collaboration between like-minded individuals or agencies is essential in order to transform an idea or opportunity into a reality. The links are not always intuitive or apparent and may come about through serendipity rather than strategy. The formation of new networks gives rise to further innovation, creating a virtuous circle of process, product or service innovation. In addition to the formation of new networks, the strengthening of extant networks is an important outcome of innovation for sustainable tourism. The case studies and analysis in this publication describe the development of networks of innovation by tourism organisations, destinations and individual entrepreneurs as part of their dynamic processes of change and transformation toward sustainability (Farrell & Twining-Ward 2005; Liburd & Carlsen 2006; Liburd & Edwards 2010).

The nature of innovation

According to Hjalager (2010) the core of the innovation concept is defined through one or more of the following six areas: product or service innovation, management innovation, process innovation, logistic innovation, market innovation and institutional innovation. These may be combined depending on the context and specific circumstances. Innovative changes are usually introduced for commercial purposes to ensure economic growth (Liburd 2005). Unless implemented as commercial elements for consumption purposes, innovations will remain economically insignificant (Schumpeter 1934). It is therefore of pivotal importance that the novelty is apparent to producers, consumers, suppliers and/or competitors. However, these cases will also illustrate the importance of social innovation processes and transformation toward more sustainable practices. Innovation is, by nature, a development process that activates a number of sub-processes and is disseminated among networks of organisations and individuals, who take up new products or practices or adjust their procedures according to the new situation. According to Trott (1998, p. 11) innovation is social: 'not a single action but a total process of interrelated sub processes. It is not just the conception of a new idea, nor the invention of a new device, nor the development of a new market. The process is all these things acting in an integrated fashion'. Indeed, networks are considered essential for fostering innovations, especially in small and medium enterprises, which predominate in the tourism sector (Lynch & Morrison 2007).

Knowledge transfer is vital to innovation and for competitiveness (Weidenfeld *et al.* 2010). In the case of EDDA (see Chapter 7) the built attraction market engaged in a process of product innovation by involving all personnel in the development of competences. Innovativeness was thereby extended from mere service and product development to include new management structures, knowledge transfer and innovative learning through network creation. Networking with a wide range of stakeholders also contributed to 'socially inclusive wealth creation' (European University Association 2007, p. 21).

Innovations in tourism enterprises are inspired and affected by a range of internal and external factors. As a means of knowledge exchange, Information Communication Technology (ICT) is often seen as a major driver of innovation (Hjalager 2010). The increasing availability and accessibility of ICT could equally be considered as a facilitator of innovation in the support of interaction, communication and dissemination of information within innovation networks. Technology facilitates the integration of a diverse range of actors that may already constitute or form a network that provides the means for innovation. In particular, the cases will show how the drive for innovation comes from individuals and organisations working together. As emphasised by Lundvall (2005, p. 13):

> *Firms, knowledge institutions and people do seldom innovate alone, and innovation emanates from cumulative processes of interactive learning and searching. This implies that the system needs to be characterized simultaneously with reference to its elements and to the relationships between those elements. The relationships may be seen as carriers of knowledge and the interaction as processes where new knowledge is produced and diffused.*

The nature of networks

Whereas Lundvall's (2005) proposition is applied in the context of innovation systems, the following will illustrate how innovation for sustainable tourism is facilitated by networks that serve as both repositories and generators of innovative ideas and information. This is especially the case with innovations that are based on user-driven methods. User-driven innovation is commonly attributed to Von Hippel (2005), who defined the concept as 'innovation created by the user to obtain a higher user value as opposed to commercial innovations taking place within companies'. Hence, the concept of user-centred innovation has literally been created by the user or customer, e.g. through social media and other forms of involvement, or through direct marketing aiming to both increase awareness and sales as well expanding the network of new customers.

Hjalager (1996) indicates that networks are an integral part of the process of innovation, which often involves 'redefinitions of interrelationships between actors' (Hjalager 1996, p. 202). These relationships may be co-operative or confrontational; both types stimulate innovation (Tremblay 2000). Hausman (2005) also finds that 'ideological innovations, such as new management practices' involve new partnerships as well as new ideas. Laing *et al.* (2008) suggest that partnerships provide a means for the diffusion of innovations. The need for partnerships for sustainable tourism in protected areas has never been greater in Australia, according to Moore *et al.* (2009). Liburd and Hergesell (2007) recognise the importance of training, education and employee retention and succession to improve learning and innovation for sustainable tourism in the European North Sea region.

Both Chesbrough (2003) and von Hippel (2005) emphasise that innovation resources are not and should not be restricted to local and close networks. Innovation networks for sustainable tourism can take many forms, as the case studies in this volume demonstrate. Some networks involve a form of horizontal integration between organisations involved in the same business: both stand to benefit from the formation of a horizontal network to support innovation. The Diablo Trust, formed by the Metzgers and the Prossers (both ranching families) in Northern Arizona (see Chapter 5), is an example of this form of innovation that leads to sustainable conservation outcomes. Family networks extend the capacity to innovate by drawing on the willingness of family members to provide additional drive and resources to achieve their goals. Innovation can commence with the founders of individual or family businesses, as demonstrated in the case of the Brenu Beach resort in Ghana (see Chapter 8) or can emerge through family interaction within and between generations (Getz, Carlsen & Morrison 2004).

Another form of innovation network is akin to vertical integration, where organisations create networks of suppliers or customers (or indeed, both) that support the dissemination through this vertical network for innovation (Hjalager 2010). A study in Bornholm, Denmark, indicated that innovation in the form of doing new things and taking risks was a factor underlying future-oriented business goals (Getz & Petersen 2002). Often, it is consumer-focused innovation that offers superior value through innovative ideas and knowledge and provides innovative firms with a strategic competitive advantage. Xanterra LLC (see Chapter 4) has established such a network of suppliers across their operations in more than 20 US national, state and marine parks to ensure that their ecological performance meets the highest standards expected by customers and Government agencies.

Other innovation networks are in the form of diagonal networks, and come about through the actions of an individual or organisation forming a previously non-existent connection with an apparently unrelated organisation in order to address a problem or pursue an opportunity that affects both organisations. AGSEP (see Chapter 9) is such an example of diagonal network formation by a German sporting organisation that aimed to achieve peace and reconciliation in ethnically divided Sri Lanka through the introduction of sport competitions. In this case, the network was the innovation that provided the drive, overcame the barriers and ensured that processes were followed.

Research framework

Our approach bears some similarity to the framework used by Hjalager *et al.* (2008), as they also considered actors, relationships and drivers in their comprehensive analysis of innovation systems in Nordic tourism. However, the approach used in this volume focuses more on the underlying processes, particularly the role of networks for innovation, rather than the outcomes of such processes.

The centrality of networks in driving innovation, facilitating processes and overcoming internal and external barriers is presented in Figure 1.1. This framework differs from Hjalager *et al.* (2008) in that it provides analysis of networks of innovation in each case, and a basis for cross-case comparison, whereas Hjalager *et al.* (2008) focus on the internal processes and external policies that lead to innovative outcomes. In subsequent work, Hjalager acknowledged that collaboration and networking are the main focus in the literature on policies that support innovation and open collaboration in various forms can foster innovation (Hjalager 2010; Liburd & Hjalager 2010, 2011).

Both approaches provide insights into the drivers of innovation, but this set of cases examines the role of networks as drivers and outcomes, whilst Hjalager *et al.* consider the role of the public sector and tourism policy and extend their framework to include wider societal and synergetic forces and other policies and institutions that drive tourism innovation. The role of networks in innovation is deemed critical, and indeed Hjalager *et al.* (2008, p. 33) considered innovation to be about 'new combinations, best fostered by dense networks of a variety of linkages'. In their model, however, networks of actors with new ways of mobilizing are seen as outcomes of the process, whereas we considered networks as important inputs to, as well as outcomes of, the innovation process.

For the purposes of this framework, networks that serve to both formulate and disseminate innovation in tourism businesses, organisations and destinations have been identified and analysed. This set of case studies provides insights into the structures, actors and relations in the respective innovation networks. It acknowledges that innovation networks have within them relational forces between actors that have 'quite different composition' (Hjalager *et al.* 2008, p. 29), This notion has direct implications for how innovation should be studied over time.

Figure 1.1 Centrality of networks for innovation

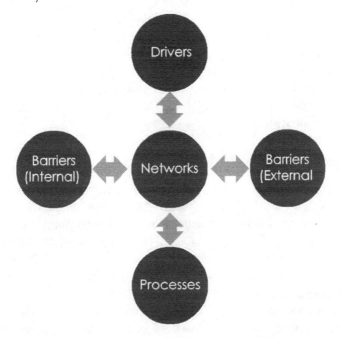

Drivers of innovation

According to Bergin-Seers, Breen and Frew (2008), innovation evolves from an innovative climate in which management plays a key role. They found eight determinants or indicators of innovative capacity that cover a number of management capabilities and behaviours:

- competent management;

- external relationship management;
- information management;
- recognition of employees;
- acknowledgement of customer relations;
- market knowledge;
- implementation of a systematic new product development process; and
- awareness of barriers.

Knowledge networks, in particular, have a key role to play in driving innovation in management of employees, relationships and customers, as well as the development of new products and systems.

In many family-owned and operated tourism businesses, family values predominate; in turn, these values influence entrepreneurial and innovative behaviour within family firms (Getz, Carlsen & Morrison 2004). Thus, it is not only important to recognise the reason for pursuit of innovation of sustainable tourism, but also to acknowledge the values underpinning those individuals, families and organisations that innovate. These values can have environmental, social and economic dimensions, or a combination of these, and can result in many actions and outcomes that constitute a shift toward sustainability. Social values can range from the higher ideals of equity and the importance of memorable experiences to the more basic human need for peace and survival. Environmental values can be focused on conservation of a single species or address the global ecological issues related to pollution and climate change. Finally, there is often an economic imperative associated with innovation that can be based on short-term opportunity or long-term strategy to develop new products, services or systems.

Overcoming barriers to innovation

Getz *et al.* (2004) found a lack of innovation among tourism and hospitality operators, due to the highly dynamic nature of tourism destinations, high rates of business turnover and ease of duplication of services in many destinations. New destinations are always emerging which are 'able to employ the latest advances in tourism management without the drag on innovation of ... staff who are used to doing things in a certain way' (Laws 2006, p. 225). High rates of business turnover and small business failure (Getz *et al.* 2004) disrupt business continuity and discourage innovation in existing firms. For many firms in tourism, imitation, as opposed to innovation, is common as they attempt to remain competitive with truly innovative firms, which in itself may act as a disincentive to innovate in the first place.

Bergin-Seers *et al.* (2006) found that the main barriers challenging the ability of tourist parks to be innovative included both internal and external factors. The external factors were local government regulations and legislation and, in particular, planning and environmental legislation. Government taxes relating to land purchases also caused great concern. Governmental red tape was an issue for tourist parks located on large areas of land requiring redevelopment. Various strategies were implemented to meet government requirements, yet progress and change were often delayed. Internal barriers were often related to the limited financial resources of the parks and their inability to tap into sources of finance. A limited number of employees and long working hours for operators made it difficult for parks to seize opportunities when they arose and restricted their ability to put in extra effort beyond day-to-day operations. Finally, some operators' lack of business experience and professional development impeded innovation, particularly when outside support was not sought. These barriers could be broadly classified as 'internal' (knowledge, financial, human resources, business) and 'external' (legislative/political, environmental, social, technological) and are encountered at some point in each of the case studies of innovation.

Processes of innovation

Most innovation processes in tourism are incremental, as opposed to disruptive 'breakthrough' innovations. Incremental innovation is characterised by steady improvement and following cultural routines and norms. It can be rapidly implemented, producing immediate gains and developing customer loyalty (Schaper & Volery 2007). Importantly, these processes are based on sustaining technologies that already exist and are easily adapted for tourism use, as described in a number of case studies in this publication. Regardless of the process of innovation, it 'remains fundamentally an application of knowledge' (Schaper & Volery 2007, p. 64). This application emphasises the role of knowledge networks in the process of innovation for sustainable tourism.

According to Kirsch (2012): 'In order to support organisations in successfully managing change and achieving the shift towards a more sustainable economy, a new paradigm is needed that looks at the complex interrelationships of individuals, organisations, organisational networks, institutions and regulatory frameworks from a systemic and procedural perspective'. Innovation for sustainable tourism requires organisations and destinations to manage change as a gradual and complex process involving individuals and networks at every stage in the process.

Case study research

Cases typically start with an introduction that sets the scene of the particular dilemma or opportunity situation that was faced by an individual, group or organisation. This is normally followed by a detailed description of the business environment and relevant circumstances that enveloped the case. A discussion of associated management decisions and processes that were relevant to the dilemma or opportunity is highlighted next. Finally, a summary/conclusion invites the reader to suggest how they would tackle the dilemma/opportunity if they were in a position to influence the necessary decisions. To assist teaching staff, cases usually include case notes that provide a brief description of the case writer's perception of the 'real' dilemma/opportunity and notes on how the actual individual, group or organisation addressed the dilemma/opportunity. All of the subsequent case studies address the following key questions:

1. Why do organisations innovate?

2. What are the key features and drivers of innovation within organisations?

3. What are the internal and external barriers to innovation that organisations face?

4. How do organisations innovate? What processes are associated with innovation?

5. How important are networks for innovation?

Contributors were encouraged to offer descriptions of innovation that would be of interest to an international audience. The resulting case studies could be considered as a convenience sample, that is, a sample design based on information gathered from members of a population who are conveniently accessible to the researcher (Jennings 2001). The review process led to a selection of ten cases (four from the US, two from Europe, and one each from Australia, Ghana, Sri Lanka and China).

Contributors were asked to consider why innovation was undertaken, what barriers were faced, how innovation was realised, and the importance of networks. Given the disparate range of contributions, it is not possible to generalise from these cases. However, indicative themes on the topic of innovation emerged from the literature and cases. Four themes were identified with reference to the drivers, barriers, processes and networks associated with each case and were analysed using a cross-case analysis approach. Cross-case analysis is a means of grouping together common responses to interviews, as well as analysing different perspective on central issues (Patton 1990; Carlsen & Getz 2001; Getz, Carlsen & Morrison 2004). Cross-case analysis begins with writing a descriptive case for each unit studied, then moves to grouping responses together according to questions, themes or central issues. In this way the issues that emerge in the case studies are integrated within the descriptive analytical framework that provides the basis for comparison and contrast.

Overview of case studies

Chapter 2 is a case study of innovation in the Scandic hotel chain, one of the largest hotel chains in Scandinavia. The managerial decision to engage in sustainability was undertaken in the early 1990s in an attempt to distinguish the company from its main competitors. Nowadays, Scandic enjoys a unique position of being a pioneer of many successful actions. These range from responsible construction, management and operation of hotels, educating team members in various sustainability-related issues and taking part in local community events, to banning jumbo prawns from all its kitchens because of unsustainable farming practices. Swedish Scandic was the first in Scandinavia to serve fair-trade coffee in all its hotels, to have a disability coordinator, and to eco-certify all hotels in a country with the Nordic Swan label. A decade of comprehensive work has allowed Scandic team members and management to learn a number of valuable lessons which, when shared with others in the sector, could greatly contribute to the greening of this industry. All these actions had no negative effect on the bottom line. On the contrary, they considerably contributed to the profitability of the company, which is now actively pursuing opportunities to expand its innovation network.

In Chapter 3, Ecocean, a not-for-profit conservation association registered in Australia, is studied. Ecocean's primary aim is to generate public awareness for marine conservation issues and include increased protection for the threatened whale shark. Whale sharks are a rare species that inhabit warm temperate and tropical ocean regions and are exposed to significant fishing pressure. They appear to be highly migratory, but congregate where seasonal 'food pulses' occur, such as the annual aggregation at Ningaloo Marine Park. Lucrative ecotourism business operations revolving around these regular annual appearances are well established at Ningaloo and several other locations worldwide. However, despite their rarity and tourism popularity, very little is known about the whale shark, which has little protection internationally. To address this, Ecocean developed an innovative system enabling whale shark identification using photos taken by tourists swimming with the sharks. Tourists upload their own photos to the Ecocean website (www.whaleshark.org). The system uses NASA star mapping technology to map whale shark skin spot patterns. Mapping unique natural skin patterning enables individuals to be identified along with their sex, age, size and other information. This information can be used to gain greater understanding of whale shark ecology and behaviour, contributing to more effective conservation and sustainable whale shark tourism operations. Use of tourist photos and an internet interface that can be customised to track sightings of specific whale sharks helps build public support for their conservation. The Ecocean case study is a story of innovation through lateral thinking and making seemingly unrelated connections.

Chapter 4 is a case study of Xanterra LLC, which operates as the US's largest national park concessionaire. It has about 8000 employees operating hotels, lodges, restaurants, retail, campgrounds and transportation systems in more than 20 locations across the US. This case study describes the innovative Environmental Management System (EMS) developed in recent years by Xanterra LLC. Innovation by Xanterra is reviewed across the full range of their operations, including accommodation, transportation, food and beverages, tour operations, energy, water and waste management. This case study provides insight into a successful and innovative company that is leading the way to sustainable practices, and serves as an example to other organisations seeking to improve their environmental management and performance.

Chapter 5 is a study of the Diablo Trust and Rural Planning Area, a Northern Arizona collaborative grassroots land management group with an innovative approach to land protection in the Diablo Canyon Rural Planning Area (RPA). Through networking with all a range of stakeholders, including local, state and federal agencies, community and conservation groups, the two long-time farming families that live beside Diablo Canyon have taken considerable steps to improve land management practices, conserve habitat for wildlife, maintain their farming traditions and ensure that the land remains representative of all of the values associated with America's West for future generations to experience.

Chapter 6 is a case study of Tasting Arizona, a consortium of tourism, non-government, indigenous, farming, education, community, festival and food organisations that aim to provide 'local flavour' in Arizona. Their belief is that consumers and visitors want local flavour, and they have identified a range of food products that represent the taste and feel of Arizona. Wild foods such as flour made from the Mesquite bean and pure varieties of fruit and vegetables are just two examples of traditional local foods that have been revived. The benefits of this revival extend well beyond providing visitors with local flavours, as these foods are linked with preserving traditional farming practices, conserving areas for wildlife, educating youth, keeping food pure and free from genetic modification, maintaining biodiversity and protecting cultural traditions.

Chapter 7 studies the Experience Development of Danish Attractions (EDDA), a project which aims to sustain the socioeconomic wellbeing of built attractions in Denmark by capitalising on the trend toward a user-oriented, experience-driven economy. Encouraging product and management innovations through joint competence development, 38 built attractions of varying size, thematic focus and ownership structure took part in the four-year initiative. Facing several economic and knowledge-related challenges, a practical approach to innovation was adopted. All personnel were involved in courses, study trips and experiential discussion groups in order to facilitate implementation of newly acquired knowledge and tools for innovation.

Chapter 8 comes from Ghana, where small and medium ecotourism businesses have been established either in isolation, around large co-operate hotels, or close to the beach, game reserves or recreational parks. These businesses are either community-based or individually owned. This case study looks at the underlying narratives that influence the innovative approaches applied in the planning, organisation and managing of an environmentally linked business in Ghana. The research investigates the underlying reasons, motivations and barriers relating to the establishment of these tourism businesses and their influence on local entrepreneurs' innovative ideas. This case study features a female entrepreneur who has tried to realise her innovative ecotourism ideas over the past five years against the background of marital problems, social status disadvantages and interferences from local government authorities.

Chapter 9 is set in Sri Lanka, where social sport events have been used to combine people's travel experiences with the emotional factor of contributing to the advancement of intercultural understanding and peace in the ethnically divided country. This innovative move by the Asian German Sports Exchange Programme (AGSEP), a non-governmental-organization (NGO) which has been conducting sport events and international exchanges between Sri Lankan and European sport teams since 1989, has resulted in positive economic, social and cultural development for the participating communities, local tourism operators and the event organiser. The international and interethnic networks created over the years are key factors which have assisted stakeholders to overcome internal and external barriers to innovation.

Chapter 10 draws on the application of innovation and resilience to tourism in a relatively conservative community setting in the Blackstone Valley in Rhode Island, USA. The Blackstone Valley Tourism Commission created the Sustainable Tourism Laboratory (STL) to identify new ways of utilizing tourism in creating resilient communities: communities that are able to flow with and prosper from today's social, economic and ecological challenges. Though still in its infancy, the STL is starting to apply complex adaptive system methods through resilience thinking and a resilient community process as a basis for its theory and practice.

Chapter 11 is a case study of Wenhai Ecolodge, a community-operated retreat run by 56 local households with support from the US-based Nature Conservancy. The case study describes the successful development of community-based tourism innovations for sustainable destination management in China. Every household purchased shares and contributed start-up financing through a loan to the Wenhai Ecolodge. The Ecolodge uses sustainable energy systems to decrease the impact on the surrounding resources. Ten percent of the lodge's profits go to a conservation and community development fund that supports projects around Wenhai. In 2003, Wenhai Ecolodge was named one of the World's Ten Best Ecolodges by *Outside Magazine*. The purpose of this case study is first to provide recommendations proposed through telephone interviews with the local residents of Wenhai Ecolodge in support of environmental restoration. Second, it is an attempt to provide a framework of analysis illuminating some of the issues inherent in sustainable tourism destination management in today's complex world.

Learning from case studies

Case studies that describe particular experiences seek to provide deep insight into local dilemmas and ignite reflection that offers valuable learning. Scholars search case studies to find inspiration and leads that improve theory. Practitioners often appreciate that peer experience can inspire and improve personal practice. Students may enjoy thinking about how they would have tackled the situation. Therefore, these cases are expected to be utilised by readers in a manner that meets their personal preferences. The intended reader variety posed a problem for the editors when presentation and summarisation was considered. For example, structuring cases into a specific format that assisted one type of reader (i.e. students) would inconvenience other readers. As the cases were written by practitioners, their peers are expected to find them useful. Researchers may require more detail and this could be obtained upon request to case authors. Case notes have been provided (see Chapter 12) to assist students looking for ideas on how to enhance their reflection. A few of the innovation cases can also be found on the Web 2.0 platformm, INNOTOUR, (www.innotour.com), where further dialogue between different user groups is encouraged.

Summary

The ten case studies in the following chapters are drawn from diverse settings and situations. The contexts and networks within which innovation is occurring are different in almost every case. The Xanterra, Scandic and EDDA cases demonstrate the challenges of implementing innovation across complex networks of organisations. Xanterra manages a large number of US national park concessions and manages an extensive network of suppliers; Scandic owns a large network of Scandinavian hotels; and the EDDA project is designed to encourage a network of 38 Danish built attractions to engage all of their personnel in product innovation. Case studies of Wenhai Ecolodge, Brenu Beach Resort and AGSEP describe the determination necessary to realise objectives in situations where network structures are evolving. Wenhai Ecolodge is run by local households with support from the US-based Nature Conservancy; in Brenu Beach, small and medium ecotourism businesses receive limited support, but may try to establish networking links with large corporate hotels, game reserves or recreational parks; and, over many years, AGSEP is developing a network of interethnic and international groups. Case studies of the Blackstone Valley Sustainable Tourism Laboratory, Diablo Trust and Tasting Arizona demonstrate how innovation can add value to traditional activities and utilise networks and resources more sustainably. All three casess are based on grassroots community networks of people with a commitment to preserving traditional cultural practices and values through sustainable tourism. Finally, the Ecocean case demonstrates how the tourists themselves can play an important role in a network for conservation through technological innovation.

Despite their diversity in setting and context, it is possible to glean the lessons and examples from each case in terms of the drivers, barriers, processes and networks of innovation by use of cross-case analysis in the final chapter. A review of the relevant literature has provided a basis for analysing the main themes and sub-themes of innovation. It also identifies new and emergent themes: in particular, the importance of networks that drive and progress innovation. In this way, existing knowledge is validated, and generalisation of the lessons learnt from both the study and the practice of innovation is offered to students, scholars and practitioners.

References

Bergin-Seers, S, Breen, JP & Frew, EA 2008, 'The Determinants and Barriers Affecting Innovation Management in Small and Medium Tourism Enterprises (SMTEs) in the Tourist Park Sector', *Tourism Recreation Research* 33(3): 245-253.

Breen, J, Bergin-Seers, S, Roberts, L, Frew, E & Carlsen, J 2006, *Innovation and Change Management for Small and Medium Tourism Enterprises in the Tourist Park Sector*, Sustainable Tourism CRC, Griffith University, Gold Coast.

Carlsen, J & Getz, D 2001, 'Cross-case analysis of family businesses in rural tourism', in C Pforr & B Janeczko, *Proceedings of the Capitalising on Research, Conference*, University of Canberra, Canberra.

Chesbrough, HW 2003, *Open innovation. The new imperative for creating and profiting from technology*, Harvard Business School Press, Boston.

De Jong, J & Vermeulen, P 2003, 'Organising Successful New Service Development: A Literature Review', *Management Decision* 41(9): 844-858.

European University Association 2007, *Creativity in Higher Education. Report on the EUA Creativity Project 2006-2007*, EUA Publications, Brussels.

Farrell, B, & Twining-Ward, L 2005, 'Seven Steps Toward Sustainability: Tourism in the Context of New Knowledge', *Journal of Sustainable Tourism* 13(2): 109-122.

Getz, D, Carlsen, J & Morrison, A 2004, *The Family Business in Tourism and Hospitality*, CABI Publishing, Wallingford.

Getz, D & Petersen, T 2002, *Growth-oriented Entrepreneurs and Destination Competitiveness*, Paper presented at Re-Inventing The Destination conference, Dubrovnik, Croatia.

Hausman, A. 2005, 'Innovativeness Among Small Businesses: Theory and Propositions for Future Research', *Industrial Marketing Management* 34: 773-782.

Hjalager, A-M 2010, 'A review of innovation research in tourism', *Tourism Management* 31: 1-12.

Hjalager, A-M 1996, 'Tourism and the Environment: The Innovation Connection,' *Journal of Sustainable Tourism* 4(4): 201-218.

Hjalager, A-M, Huijbens, EH, Björk, P, Nordin, S, Flagestad, A & Knútsson, Ö 2008, *Innovation systems in Nordic tourism*, Nordic Innovation Centre, Oslo.

Jennings, G 2001, *Tourism Research*, Wiley, Australia.

Kandari, OP & Chandar, A 2004, *Tourism, Biodiversity and Sustainable Development*, Isha Books, New Delhi.

Kirsch, K 2012, 'Systems Theory and Organisation Change for a Sustainable Future', In G Jones, *Current Research in Sustainability*, Tilde University Press, Melbourne.

Laing, J, Wegner, A, Moore, S, Weiler, B, Pfueller, S, Lee, D, Macbeth, J, Croy, G & Lockwood, M 2008, *Developing effective partnerships for facilitating sustainable protected area tourism: Literature review*, Sustainable Tourism CRC, Gold Coast.

Laws E 2006, 'Considerations in Improving Tourism and Hospitality Service Systems', In B Prideaux, G Moscardo and E Laws (eds), *Managing Tourism and Hospitality Services: Theory and International Applications*, CABI, Wallingford: 225-236.

Liburd, JJ 2005, 'Sustainable Tourism and Innovation in Mobile Tourism Services'. *Tourism Review International* 9(1): 107-118.

Liburd, JJ & Carlsen, J 2006, 'Family Businesses and Sustainable Tourism: the role of family businesses in sustainable tourism development', in J Liburd & A Hergsell (eds), *Proceedings of the BEST Education Network Think Tank VI*, University of Girona, Girona, Spain.

Liburd, J & Hergesell, A 2007, *BEST Education Network Think Tank VII Innovations for Sustainable Tourism*. Conference proceedings. University of Technology Sydney.

Liburd, J & Edwards, D 2010, *Understanding the Sustainable Development of Tourism,* Goodfellows Publishers, Oxford.

Liburd, JJ & Hjalager, A-M 2010, 'Changing Approaches to Education, Innovation and Research – Student experiences', *Tourism Journal of Hospitality and Tourism Management* 17: 12-20.

Liburd, JJ & Hjalager, A-M 2011, 'From copyright to *copyleft.* Toward Tourism Education 2.0', in: I Ateljevic, N. Morgan & A Pritchard (eds), *The Critical Turn in Tourism Studies: Creating an Academy of Hope,* Routledge, Oxon: 96-109.

Lundvall, B-Å 2005, *Innovation system research and policy. Where it came from and where it should go,* Paper, Aalborg University, Denmark.

Moore, S, Weiler, B, Croy, G, Laing, J, Lee, D, Lockwood, M, Pfueller, S & Wegner, A 2009, *Tourism – protected area partnerships in Australia. Designing and managing for success,* Sustainable Tourism CRC: Gold Coast.

Patton, MQ 1990, *Qualitative Evaluation and Research Methods,* Sage Publications, California.

Russell, B 1996, 'Innovation in small tourism business', in R Thomas & R Shacklock (eds), *Spring Symposium Proceedings of the International Association of Hotel Management Schools,* Leeds Metropolitan University, Leeds, UK: 116-120.

Schaper, M & Volery, T 2007, Entrepreneurship and Small Business, 2nd Pacific Rim edition, Wiley, Australia.

Schumpeter, J 1934, *The theory of economic development,* Harvard, Boston.

Tremblay, P 2000, 'An Evolutionary Interpretation of the Role of Collaborative Partnerships in Sustainable Tourism', in *Tourism Collaboration and Partnerships: Politics, Practice and Sustainability,* B Bramwell & B Lane (eds), Clevedon, Channel View: 314-332.

von Hippel, E 2005, *Democratizing innovation*, MIT Press, Cambridge, Massachusetts.

Weidenfeld, A, Williams, AM & Butler, RW 2010, 'Knowledge transfer and innovation among attractions', *Annals of Tourism Research* 37(3): 604-626.

Chapter 2

Scandic Hotels

Embracing Omtanke - 'caring for each other'

PAULINA BOHDANOWICZ-GODFREY

INTRODUCTION

With more than 160 hotels in the Nordic and Northern Europe, Scandic is one of the largest hotel operators in Scandinavia. It is well established and widely recognised in most strategic tourist and business destinations in the Nordic region. As an independent company with a strong owner (equity fund, EQT Partners) behind it, Scandic is actively pursuing opportunities to expand its network in Europe. With over ten years of experience in environmental and social engagement, Scandic is a business frequently mentioned when the subject of sustainability is raised in the travel and tourism industry (Dodson 2007; JD Power & Associates 2007; Nilsson 2007; Hotels 2008).

Scandic's history dates back to 1963 and the first Esso Motor Hotel that opened in Närke, Sweden. The uniqueness of the concept and high standard offered led to an immediate success, and in the early 1990s Scandic had over 100 hotels in Scandinavia and Europe. From initial locations along motorways, the hotel network expanded to city locations. When the 1991 Kuwait crisis occurred, the impact was felt in the distant Nordic countries, requiring Scandic's management to urgently come up with a new development and business policy in order to enhance the operation and increase bookings.

Drivers of innovation

The company needed a strategy that would not only provide short-term operational gains, but also help create 'a strong brand that the employees could be proud of and guests could identify with' (Bergkvist, Vice President Sustainable Businesses at Scandic, personal communication, 22 November 2007). Following the publication of the Brundtland Report in 1987, environmental awareness was slowly reaching wider social and political agendas in Europe and Scandinavia. Consequently, in 1993 Scandic management decided to accentuate environmental engagement, according to the Natural Step principles, as the core value of the 'New Scandic'. It announced its policy 'to lead the way and work continuously to promote both a reduction in our environmental impacts and a better environment' (Nattrass & Altomare 1999; Scandic 2003). Scandic aims at achieving this 'whilst retaining or increasing comfort and customer benefit' (Nattrass & Altomare 1999; Scandic 2003; Scandic 2004a).

Soon the company saw the tangible effects of responsible operation in the form of reduced energy and water consumption and costs (Scandic 2000), as well as external recognition through environmental awards (1995 'Environmental Stand Award' and 1996 'Greening the Business' Tourism Award) and a range of future opportunities. With growing understanding of the need for sustainable development, the initial goal of environmental profiling was expanded to holistically cover all aspects of sustainability with the introduction of The Compass and the concept of Omtanke in 1998 (Bohdanowicz & Zientara 2008; Bohdanowicz & Zientara, 2009). At Scandic, Omtanke means 'caring for our guests and each other while caring for the environment and the society around us' (Scandic 2007), and The Compass shows the aspects of sustainability covered in the Scandic business model (Figure 2.1). Scandic believes 'in everybody's right to be treated equally, feel safe and be well taken care of [so called Nordic common sense]' and aims to 'offer easy and accessible travel for all (Scandic 2007). Scandic's business vision is 'To help our guests recharge their batteries, in a simple and accessible way' (Scandic 2011).

Barriers to innovation

Pioneers frequently encounter legislative, political, technological, business, environmental or social obstacles while implementing new ideas. Scandic also faced several difficulties during the implementation of its sustainability program.

At the beginning, the company had to address internal barriers, including the varying levels of knowledge and environmental awareness among its team members. To achieve this, environmental training courses were arranged, initially as classroom workshops: with time they were developed into an e-learning program, available on the Scandic intranet platform. Today, the environmental training pack is included in the 'Get on Board' section for all new employees. In addition, courses on sustainability are now organised within the framework of the internal university, Scandic Business School, while environmental coordinators meet regularly. Since the company started its focus on sustainability, over 11,000 team members were given training on sustainability issues (Scandic 2011). Equipped with knowledge on more responsible operation schemes, such as energy and water efficiency and conservation practices, Scandic was ready to put these into practice.

Figure 2.1 Compass of Scandic's core business values

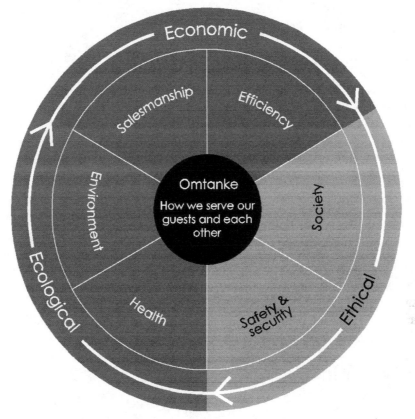

Source: Scandic 2007.

However, external barriers were encountered when external companies needed to be included in the process, especially in cases of improvements in building installations (i.e. changing the heating system or building thermo-modernisation). Scandic typically rents the building from an owner, which frequently makes it difficult to find a compromise between the goals of both stakeholders in respect to resource utilisation and necessary investments in modernisation of the building systems. Scandic thus decided to first focus on improvements that could be achieved by altering team members' behaviour, such as switching off unused equipment, conserving water during housekeeping and replacing light bulbs. Once the benefits of such actions were documented, the next step involved communication with building owners on possible co-operation in implementing technical solutions, including change of boilers and installation of heat exchangers. The dialogue continues, and many successful compromises have already been achieved. One of the most prominent successes is the co-operation between Scandic and the hotel property company Pandox, which sees the investment of 1.6 billion SEK (US$230m) in the upgrade and development of 40 of its hotels: the largest hotel investment in the Nordic region (Scandic 2011).

Many of the initiatives decided by Scandic required the co-operation of suppliers, who needed to provide products with lowered environmental impact. Few such products were available on the market, but in many instances Scandic initiated the demand for these (Bohdanowicz, Simanic & Martinac 2005). As part of this endeavour the company developed the Scandic Supplier Declaration, and asked all suppliers to document their corporate environmental policies and sign the declaration (Hardt, Environmental Coordinator at Scandic Sweden, personal communication, 17 March 2004).

At times, local or national legislation or existing contracts posed external barriers: utilities and service providers inhibited the implementation of certain initiatives, such as donation of food to charity, or recycling particular types of waste. While the regulations must be followed, individual Scandic hotels have managed to renegotiate contracts or implement alternative solutions.

The last, but certainly not least, of the internal barriers is funding. It has been widely documented that acting responsibly is profitable (Enz & Siguaw 1999; Martinac *et al.* 2001; SSCC 2003; most published best practice case studies). However, technical improvement typically requires an upfront investment and may have a long payback time (but the benefits would be long term too). This investment needs to be justified against actions in other departments, such as marketing, which may bring profits in a much shorter time. Thus, a common practice is to implement major improvements in building systems during refurbishment.

Processes for innovation

After the decision to engage in environmental issues was made, many actions followed. The first steps included the establishment of the corporate environmental policy and program based on the Natural Step principles, education and training of the team members and action plans for individual hotels (for more information see Bohdanowicz *et al.* 2005; Bohdanowicz & Zientara 2008, 2009).

The target of increasing the use efficiency and conserving natural resources was tackled within the framework of the so-called 'Resource Hunt' program, with a special online database, the Scandic Utility System (SUS), developed for the monitoring of resource consumption. Currently, the upgraded version of the database — the Scandic Sustainability Indicator Reporting (ScandicSIR) — is used. Next, the Best in the Class system (BINC, now Balance Score Card or BSC), based on SUS, was developed to measure key performance indicators. Nowadays, the 'Resource Hunt' program includes an employee reward system based on results from ScandicSIR and BSC, where monetary rewards are transferred to a special fund at the hotel and allocated for social activities of the team members.

In the next stage, committed to purchasing products with a low (lifecycle) environmental impact, Scandic decided to involve their suppliers in the environmental program, and developed the Scandic Supplier Declaration. As part of the company's attempt to reduce fossil carbon emissions to zero by 2025, all Norwegian and Swedish Scandic facilities have (since 2004) been supplied with 'green/non-fossil' electricity (SIR 2007), and the management is looking into negotiating similar contracts in other locations.

Continuous retrofitting of facilities was recognised as an excellent opportunity of further reducing environmental impact; subsequently, the Scandic Environmental Construction Standard was developed to facilitate the process of responsible decision-making. The document lists materials which may not be used in the facilities, and specifies acceptable alternatives (Scandic 2004b). To further minimise the amount of waste generated on site, the company incorporated comprehensive waste sorting and recycling programs, and eliminated the use of single packaged items where possible. The company made a step further and, rather than having four million bottles of water transported to its premises, decided to produce and bottle its own product on site. This has cut annual carbon emissions by 106 tonnes, and one SEK (US$0.23) from each bottle sold is donated to the Scandic Sustainability Fund (Scandic 2011). The annual consumption of on-site bottled water is in the range of 60,000 liters.

At the onset of the new millennium, corporate management decided to eco-certify facilities with the Nordic Swan eco-label. All Swedish Scandic hotels were Nordic Swan labelled by the end of 2004 (Mattsson, Sustainability Coordinator at Scandic Sweden, personal communication, 3 April 2008). Currently, four out of five Scandic hotels are eco-certified with Nordic Swan, and works continue to have all of them labelled in the next few years (Scandic 2011). Properties outside of the Nordic region work towards the EU Flower label. Every hotel has a team member with responsibility for the environment, and their goal is to facilitate participation of individual hotels in various activities and provide feedback on facility performance to the team members.

As part of its sustainability commitment, Scandic launched a 'Scandic in Society' program aiming to contribute to the wellbeing of societies in which the company operates (Bohdanowicz & Zientara 2008). Following dialogue with the team members, community programs were created in each hotel, with particular focus on those activities that are based on personal involvement. Furthermore, having recognised the growing number of people with various disabilities who want to lead a normal life and be accommodated in hotels, Scandic was among the first companies to appoint a Disability Coordinator (2003) and to create a checklist (Scandic Accessibility Standard) to make hotels accessible to all customers. This 110-point checklist applies to all hotels and is an integral consideration for all products and services offered (Berglund, Disability Coordinator at Scandic Sweden, personal communication, 1 November 2007).

The environmental commitment and performance of the company has for many years been communicated to guests and the general public through a number of channels, such as the 'Environmental Corner', hotel TV, notices displayed in various parts of hotel rooms, the company webpage and annual reports. But 2007 saw a campaign solely dedicated to documenting a decade of the company's sustainability engagement, 'Scandic Better World'. There were posters and notices displayed in all hotels, and the information on Scandic's environmental performance was included on the back side of the hotel bill (Figure 2.2). In addition, an 'Omtanke' book, presenting 24 hours in the life of a hotel from a sustainability perspective, was published, and a special web page was designed, not only documenting the achievements of the company but also providing tips and ideas for people to apply in their own homes (www.scandichotels.com/betterworld).

Networks for innovation

Scandic specialises in offering hospitality services to customers, not in sustainability or environmental protection. It is enough that management acknowledges its limited knowledge in certain areas and seeks external expertise. To access this knowledge network, Scandic, in 1994, entered into a partnership with Dr Karl-Henrik Robèrt and developed Scandic's environmental program 'The Environmental Dialogue', based on The Natural Step principles (Nattrass & Altomare 1999; Scandic 2003; Bohdanowicz *et al.* 2005). Dr Robèrt continues to assist Scandic in its sustainability endeavors, supporting it with knowledge and innovative concepts and solutions.

Throughout the years, there were a few consulting companies and individuals assisting to shape the sustainability programs at Scandic. Eco-certification of facilities with ISO Type I label (Nordic Swan and EU Flower), and purchase of KRAV-labelled food (the entire breakfast buffet in Sweden is KRAV-labelled) and fair trade coffee can also be viewed as networking, helping the company implement innovative solutions and further ensuring the validity of end results. Other partnerships, such as membership in the International Business Leaders Forum (IBLF) International Tourism Partnership, are based on mutual exchange of know-how. Others focus on implementing innovative solutions in areas outside of Scandic's business (funder of the Stockholm Water Prize, and support for Pink Ribbon International campaign). In 2009, Scandic entered a unique partnership with internationally celebrated chef Jamie Oliver to develop menus for different target groups within Scandic's customer base (Scandic 2009).

Within the 'Scandic in Society' program, individual hotels frequently enter into partnerships with local authorities and non-governmental organisations (NGOs) to find innovative solutions for local community problems. Co-operation with schools and universities is also common, where students suggest more sustainable alternatives to current modes of hotel operation.

Many awards presented to Scandic may also be considered a network for innovation, as recognition in a particular area of activity promotes the initiative and may help other companies implement better practices. The awards include the 1999 'European Design & Development Award' for the eco-room concept, the

Figure 2.2 The back side of the hotel room bill

	10 things to make your home a little bit more like a Scandic:
1)	Change to compact fluorescent light bulbs.
2)	Buy organic, eco-labelled products. Buy in bulk.
3)	Reduce. Reuse. Recycle.
4)	Use renewable energy for your home.
5)	Use high-efficiency applicances, shut off completely when not is use.
6)	Reduce and replace cleaners with eco-labelled ones. Reduce water use.
7)	Become more involved in your community.
8)	Replace fossil fuel vehicles with bicycles, mass transport, hybrid or flexi-fuel.
9)	Minimise your carbon emissions.
10)	Buy all-natural, preferably ec-labelled textiles, wood flooring and furniture.

Thanks to you, the world is becoming more sustainable.

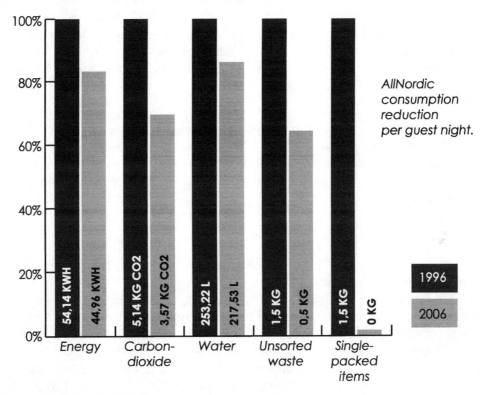

Source: Scandic, April 2007.

2002 'IH&RA Environmental Award', the 2006 St. Julian Prize for accessibility, the 2007 SLEEP 'Sustainability Award' and the 2007 MKG Hospitality 'Best CSR Programme Award'. In 2008, Scandic received the Silver 'Tourism for Tomorrow

Award' and Gold 'IMEX Green Meetings' award. 2011 saw Sandic receive 'The Nordic Council and Nature Environmental' prize.

Yet another network for innovation took form when Scandic was a part of the Hilton Group PLC (later Hilton Worldwide). Scandic served as a role model in the area of environmental initiatives. A number of ideas originating from Scandic were incorporated into Hilton's European environmental program, following modifications of various degrees. Among the solutions adopted by Hilton were the 'eco-learning' program, an interactive environmental training based on the Four Steps, and the Hilton Environmental Reporting database developed from the Scandic Utility System. It may be concluded that Scandic had a positive influence on the environmental management of the Hilton operations in Europe and triggered some permanent pro-environmental behavioural changes within the company.

The Scandic Sustainability Fund is one of the most unique networks for innovation established by Scandic. The Fund was initiated in 2009 and is fed by donations from the sale of on-site bottled water at Scandic hotels as well as from the sales of the single recorded by Martin Stenmarck especially for Scandic. One krona (1SEK = US$0.23) from every carafe sold is donated to the fund and amounts to about 1 million SEK a year (about US$154,000). The Fund is open to projects of a type not already part of Scandic's regular business. The company is looking for innovative partners in the fields of social commitment and the environment. Projects submitted must be innovative, not yet established and applicable in the hotel world, as well as focusing on making the world a better place to live.

Scandic continues to enter into partnerships and create and expand networks for innovation. However, after a decade of comprehensive sustainability work, Scandic team members and management are in the position to share the expertise they gained with others in the hotel sector, which could greatly contribute to the greening of this industry.

Summary

The activities undertaken by Scandic over the years represent a comprehensive approach to the issue of sustainability. As a pioneer, Scandic faced a number of obstacles, but the common belief held by management and team members that the direction was correct allowed the process to continue. Corporate determination and collective efforts paid off, not only in monetary terms, but also in a long-term perspective in the creation of a widely recognised brand. The Scandic brand is associated with social and environmental values by the team members and the customers alike. Its focus on sustainability earned it the 2008 Silver Tourism for Tomorrow Award, one of the most regarded sustainability accolades in the industry. The economic savings are also important, and since the implementation of the 'Resource Hunt' program, the 'avoided costs' from reductions in resource consumption add up to millions of dollars. In environmental terms, the average per guest-night energy and water consumption at Scandic Nordic was reduced by

21 percent and 16 percent respectively; between 1996 and 2007, carbon dioxide emissions dropped by 34 percent and unsorted waste by 66 percent.

Although currently many companies tend to profile themselves as 'green', the decision taken by Scandic in the early 1990s was both innovative and brave. The implementation of the concept of 'Omtanke - caring for each other', highlighted as the focal point of the company development policy and strongly supported by the management and the team members, proved to be timely and successful from a marketing as well as an economic point of view.

References

Bohdanowicz, P, Simanic, B & Martinac, I 2005, 'Environmental training and measures at Scandic Hotels, Sweden', *Tourism Review International* 9(1): 7-19.

Bohdanowicz ,P & Zientara, P 2009, 'Hotel companies' contribution to improving the quality of life of local communities and the well-being of their employees', Tourism and Hospitality Research 9(2): 147-158.

Bohdanowicz, P & Zientara, P 2008, 'Corporate Social Responsibility in Hospitality: Issues and Implications. - Case Study of Scandic', Scandinavian Journal of Hospitality and Tourism 8(4): 271-293

Dodson, S 2007, 'Nordic hotel chain cuts carbon footprint by a third', *Guardian Unlimited*, August 31, accessed November 26 2007, www.guardian.co.uk/travel/2007/aug/31/travelnews.hotels1.

Enz, CA & Siguaw, JA 1999, 'Best hotel environmental practices', *The Cornell Hotel and Restaurant Administration Quarterly* 40(5): 72-77.

Hotels Magazine 2008, Front cover, January 2008.

JD Power & Associates 2007, *2007 European hotel guest satisfaction index (EGSI) study*, JD Power & Associates, Westlake Village, USA.

Martinac, I, Murman, H & Lind af Hageby, A 2001, *Energy-efficiency and environmental management in a Swedish conference facility – case study: Sånga- Säby Courses & Conferences.* Proceedings of the 18th Conference on Passive and Low Energy Architecture – PLEA 2001, November 7-9, 2001, Florianópolis, Brazil: 325-329.

Nattrass, B & Altomare, M 1999, *The Natural Step for businesses: Wealth, ecology and the evolutionary corporation*, New Society Publishers, Gabriola Island, BC.

Nilsson, K 2007, 'Vi har ett miljoforsprang', *Svenska Dagbladet*, July 7, Stockholm, Sweden: 6.

Scandic 2000, *Annual report 1999*, Scandic Hotels AB, Stockholm, Sweden.

Scandic 2003, *Environmental common sense – that's sustainability in practice*, Scandic AB and Hilton International Nordic Region, Stockholm, Sweden.

Scandic 2004a, Scandic company web page, accessed July 14, 2004, www.scandic-hotels.com.

Scandic 2004b, *Scandic environmental refurbishment equipment and construction standard (SERECS): Sustainable construction and refurbishment at Scandic* (3rd edn), Scandic AB, Hilton International Nordic Region, Stockholm, Sweden.

Scandic 2007, *Omtanke – a day in the life of a Scandic hotel*, Scandic, Stockholm, Sweden.

Scandic 2009, *Jamie Oliver and Scandic in unique partnership*, news release, 17 January, Scandic, Stockholm, Sweden.

Scandic 2011, Scandic company web page, accessed September 30, 2011, www.scandichotels.com.

Scandic Better World 2011, Scandic Better World Campaign web page, accessed September 1, 2011, www.scandic-campaign.com.

SIR 2007, Scandic Sustainabililty Indicator Reporting database, accessed November 21, 2007 (For confidentiality reasons the webpage URL cannot be revealed).

SSCC 2003, *Sånga Säby Miljö redovisning 2002* (Environmental report - in Swedish), Sånga Säby Kurs och Konference, Svårtsjö, Sweden.

Chapter 3

Ecocean

Conservation through technological innovation

Michael Hughes

INTRODUCTION

Ecocean is a not-for-profit organisation initially established and managed by Brad Norman. Brad Norman has postgraduate qualifications in marine biology and began studying whale sharks at Ningaloo Marine Park in Western Australia in 1994. He set up Ecocean in 1999 with a continuing focus on facilitating marine ecosystem research and generating public awareness for marine conservation issues. After encountering the whale shark in the Ningaloo Reef region of Western Australia, Brad Norman developed a strong interest in researching and conserving the vulnerable species.

Even though it is the focus for significant 'swim with the whale shark' tourism operations, very little is known about whale shark biology, including its life cycle and preferred breeding habitats. This, in part, is due to difficulties in gathering data on whale shark biology and behaviour without lethal means. It also historically relates to the difficulties in gaining a broader understanding of the species owing to disconnected sighting locations and minimal understanding of migration routes and patterns (Holmberg *et al.* 2009). Ecocean recognised a need to establish a non-invasive method for generating sound scientific data for identification and tracking of whale sharks. This would facilitate greater understanding and awareness of the species and contribute to better conservation and management. Ecocean actively lobbies for the development of international conservation management measures and identification of areas of ecological significance for whale sharks (Ecocean, no date). This case study looks at how

Ecocean innovated to provide a practical means for non-invasive research into whale shark habits, biology and ecology. The knowledge gained through such innovation makes a vital contribution toward the conservation of whale sharks and the sustainability of the tourism businesses that rely on them.

Ecocean's primary interests include increased protection for the vulnerable whale shark based on research and advocacy. The approach revolves around gathering data on whale shark behaviour and biology. Whale sharks are classified as a vulnerable species by the International Union for Conservation of Nature (IUCN), and inhabit warm temperate and tropical ocean regions. They can grow to up to 18 metres in length but are more commonly sighted at between eight and ten metres in length. Whale sharks filter-feed on small marine organisms such as krill, jellyfish and marine animal larvae. They appear to be highly migratory, and can inhabit both deep ocean and shallow coastal areas. Whale sharks tend to congregate where seasonal 'food pulses' occur. For example, the predictable whale shark aggregation at Ningaloo Marine Park in Western Australia is closely linked with feeding opportunities associated with increased productivity in the region associated with mass coral spawning (Norman & Stevens 2007). Lucrative ecotourism operations, providing 'swim with whale shark' experiences, revolving around these annual appearances are well established at Ningaloo Marine Park and several other locations worldwide. Whale shark–based tourism contributes significantly to the economy in these regions (Arzoumanian *et al.* 2005; Caitlin *et al.* 2010).

Despite their vulnerable species status and popularity as a tourism attraction, the whale shark has very little coordinated protection internationally. Very few of the 100 countries where this species is known to visit have conservation management measures in place. There are no international programs to protect habitat for this migratory species, and no immediate plans to identify and protect areas of significance such as breeding grounds. Such conservation practices are common. International treaties, such as the Ramsar Convention on Wetlands and the UN World Heritage Area program, provide a framework for international co-operation for conservation of particular unique or significant natural phenomena. In the absence of such a treaty, the whale shark is exposed to considerable pressure from hunting and other human activities that may disturb habitat. There is evidence that hunting of whale sharks is resulting in a decline in the population. The evidence is based on an apparent decrease in the number of sighted juveniles. In response, several nations have moved to ban hunting of whale sharks. The Philippines banned all hunting and commercial trade of whale shark products in 1998. India instigated a similar ban in 2001, while Taiwan followed suit in 2007 (Whale Shark and Oceanic Research Centre 2010). The threats to whale shark populations and the reported decline in sightings of larger individuals has provided added impetus toward gathering data on whale sharks to enable appropriate measures to be taken for their conservation (Rolex Awards 2006).

In relation to the need to understand migration patterns to inform conservation efforts, research supported by Ecocean demonstrated that whale sharks have individually unique spot patterns on their skin. Thus, taking images of whale sharks at known locations and times should, in theory, allow tracking of individual sharks geographically and over time by comparing spot patterns. Using photographic images in this way would provide a practical and non-invasive method for identifying sharks and gathering data. The use of skin patterns to identify individual animals is a common practice. However, the method that Ecocean devised for such analysis is highly innovative.

Figure 3.1 Whale shark photography

Source: Hessburg, J & Hessburg, S 2009, Honudras, Utila Island: The exciting Utila Aggressor. US Dive Travel Network. Accessed Dec 17, 2007 at: www.usdivetravel.com/ V-HONDURAS-UtilaAggressor.html.

Drivers of innovation

In this case, innovation was driven by a need to comparatively analyse large quantities of photographic data efficiently and accurately. This led Ecocean to the resulting collaboration with NASA. Having identified the unique skin spot patterns of whale sharks as a possible means for identifying individuals, Ecocean commenced gathering images of whale sharks for analysis. As a means for gathering visual recordings of whale shark sightings from around the world, an online library of images accessible to whale shark tourists was created. This was one of the first applications of the Shepherd Project.

The Shepherd Project aimed to support wildlife research data collection and centralisation. Its main goal was the creation of a Web-based catalogue framework for the management of mark–recapture data accumulated by a global research community (Arzoumanian 2005). When applied by Ecocean, the system enabled individuals around the globe to upload their photographs of whale sharks to the online library, resulting in the accumulation of a very large number of whale shark images. The objective was to gather images of whale sharks over time and across geographical areas. Identifying repeated sightings of the same animal was an essential step in mapping movements of individuals and understanding their characteristics over time.

The common method for matching photos of individual animals using skin patterns was a manual exercise. This involved comparing images using measurements and judgment. However, the rapidly growing number of uploaded images created difficulties in matching individual sharks and keeping track of repeat sightings manually (Rolex Awards 2006).

> ... *we used to ... try to match them up by eye but as you're getting thousands and thousands of photos into the library it's just, it's impossible (Brad Norman,* Catalyst *transcript, ABC TV, 8 November 2007).*

A system was required for processing the thousands of images efficiently and reliably in order to analyse the visual data and generate meaningful and useful knowledge about whale sharks' behaviour and biology. The ability to identify repeated sightings of individual sharks over time and in different geographical places provides knowledge regarding migration patterns, age, growth rates and differences between males and females. Such information may be used to inform effective conservation management plans and the establishment of marine reserves to protect breeding grounds and food sources for the whale shark. Such action could contribute significantly to halting the decline in whale shark numbers.

Barriers to innovation

External barriers to achieving the goals of this project initially related to gaining recognition for the importance of conserving whale sharks. This stymied access to adequate funding for conservation and promotion activities. It was necessary to build interest in whale shark research in order to access funds to develop the project. Initially, Brad Norman carried out his work using sporadic funding from research grants coupled with his own financial backing. Marine research is costly, owing to the reliance on expensive technical equipment and the operational costs of running a research vessel in a remote region of Western Australia. National and international campaigns for the whale shark's conservation were launched with eventual success in terms of gaining support and recognition (Rolex Awards 2006). Two cash awards for innovation (Rolex Award and Duke's Choice Award) enabled Norman to devote more time to the project.

Once Norman was established as a recognised whale shark expert and conservationist, the development of an online whale shark image library presented new internal challenges in the processing of data. The enthusiastic response from whale shark tourists resulted in about 1500 images being uploaded to the library by 2007. By 2012, the database had accumulated over 39,000 photographic images based on 17,000 sightings of whale sharks around the world, and more than 3,500 whale sharks have been collaboratively tagged, based on data from over 3,200 contributors (Ecocean 2012).

The increasing number of images created another barrier of a technical nature for Ecocean. The established manual method for matching sightings of animals with spot patterns by eye was not viable for the huge quantity of whale shark images submitted to the Ecocean library. A method was required to enable large-scale automatic analysis that provided reliable results. Initially, developing such a method was beyond the expertise and resources of Ecocean.

Processes for innovation

The innovative approach to image analysis evolved from a combination of need and fortuitous circumstance. The seeds of innovation came from the establishment of the online image library and the enthusiastic response from tourists. The website was very successful in terms of rapidly collecting a large number of images. However, the quantity and varying quality of images presented difficulties in terms of efficient matching and identification of repeat sightings of individual sharks.

The next step towards the innovative analysis technique came through a chance meeting and a subsequent international professional network. In 2002, American computer engineer Jason Holmberg contacted Brad Norman and agreed to help organise and automate the Ecocean image database. Holmberg became interested in whale sharks after an encounter during a dive and eventually made contact with Brad Norman seeking more information. Faced with the problem of comparing and matching a large number of photographic images, Holmberg explained the image matching problem to a NASA-affiliated astronomer, Zaven Arzoumanian. A colleague of Arzoumanian, Gijs Nelemans, identified a technique used by Hubble Space Telescope scientists for mapping star patterns, known as the Groth algorithm, as having potential to solve the problem. After considerable work refining the algorithm for use on a living creature, a reliable way to identify individuals in virtually any spotted animal population was developed (Rolex Awards 2006).

> … we highlight the different spots behind the gills, and it's actually the angles between all those spots, we use. We triangulate. As the shark grows, the spots will move also but the angle between each spot doesn't change and that's the system we use and that's what's so unique about our project. … It scans against thousands of other photos and it comes up with the top possibilities… (Brad Norman, Catalyst interview transcript, ABC TV, 8 November 2007).

The adaptation of the algorithm attracted an award from the software manufacturer Sun Systems, which cited it as 'a very unique use of servlet-applet communication…' (Java.com 2005). This innovation came from the ability to think laterally, accessing knowledge and skills from contacts from apparently unrelated fields of expertise and applying them to a practical problem.

Figure 3.2 Computer image analysis of whale shark skin spots

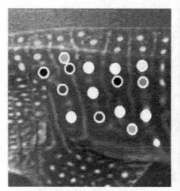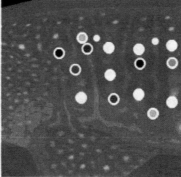

Source: Ecocean website photo ID library page 'Photographing a whale shark'. Accessed Dec 17, 2007 at http://www.whaleshark.org/photographing.jsp?langCode=es.

Networks for innovation

Ecocean's efforts to establish a greater understanding of the global marine environment have received acknowledgement and support from local, national and international groups, generating a global support network. Winning several awards raised awareness of the project and created interest and opportunities for further international involvement in photographing the sharks. Increased recognition also resulted in increased backing for the project through financial awards and grants. This effectively created an international network of data-gathering tourists and support and interest from various government and non-government groups.

> *Anybody in the world that might happen to see a whale shark whether it be diving or on an Eco-Tour or even fishing they can take a photo and actually help with our understanding of whale sharks on an international scale (Catalyst interview transcript, ABC TV, 8 November 2007).*

The professional network established through the meeting of Brad Norman and Jason Holmberg was the key to developing the image analysis innovation. It is reported that Holmberg was reminded of star patterns when viewing the whale shark skin spots and so he contacted a friend and astrophysicist working at NASA, Zaven Arzoumanian. Arzoumanian was reticent about the possibility of spot pattern matching using software. However, a colleague of his, Gijs Nelemans, assured him that star pattern matching algorithms existed and could be adapted for use on animals. Holmberg and Arzoumanian were able to obtain and modify an algorithm that had been developed in 1986 for star mapping. Skin pattern matching had normally been done manually (e.g. for cheetahs, giraffes and zebras) but required many hours of comparisons and measurements by wildlife experts of images of varying quality. The modification of the 1986 algorithm required considerable effort but eventually enabled rapid matching of whale shark skin pattern images. This greatly facilitated the ability to identify repeat sightings of individual animals from a large database of images (Bazilchuk 2006). The system has great potential for adaptation to other animal image databases that rely on identification by skin spot patterns. The development of this innovation was a combination of a chance meeting, development of international interest in whale shark research, recruitment of tourists as neo–research assistants, and the ability to make use of contacts with interested individuals working in NASA.

Summary

The innovative techniques of data gathering and analysis have enabled a better understanding of whale sharks and their movements. For example, recent complex analysis of the accumulated photographic data suggests that the numbers of whale sharks at Ningaloo Reef is not in decline as previously thought. However, the average size of whale sharks sighted appears to be reduced, indicating that there is a increased proportion of younger whale sharks frequenting Ningaloo Reef (Holmberg *et al.* 2009). The findings point to the need for more research into population dynamics, reproduction and migration patterns to understand the significance of these results in the context of whale shark population dynamics.

The Ecocean case study is a story of innovation through lateral thinking and making seemingly unrelated connections. Ecocean is an organisation highly motivated to research, raise awareness of and work to preserve whale sharks, a rare marine animal. This has been operationalised through building personal, public, non-governmental organisation and government agency support. Lobbying to establish national and international conservation measures for whale sharks has engaged governments. Accessing tourists as whale shark researchers built public support and awareness. The approach also functioned as an efficient, cost-effective means of collecting information on a global scale. The development of the whale shark online image library was a core component of the success of this approach, enabling tourists encountering whale sharks to contribute their images for research. The image analysis approach was made viable by adapting and applying software originally designed for the Hubble Space Telescope.

The development of the innovative photographic image analysis tool was the result of both full commitment to a plan based on hard work and fortuitous circumstance. While the meeting of Brad Norman and Jason Holmberg may be a chance occurrence, the ability to recognise the opportunity for application of seemingly unconnected resources demonstrates the power of lateral thinking. Ultimately, the image analysis software that enabled the whale shark image library to viably perform its function resulted from the key players recognizing opportunities and applying lateral thinking to make connections between apparently unrelated things to solve a problem.

References

Arzoumanian, Z, Holmberg, J & Norman, B 2005, 'An astronomical pattern- matching algorithm for computer-aided identification of whale sharks. Rhinocodon typus', *Journal of Applied Ecology* 42(6): 999-1011.

Bazilchuk, N 2006, 'Using pattern matching tools from astrophysics for shark conservation', *Conservation in Practice* 7(2): 35-36.

Caitlin, J, Jones, T, Norman, B & Wood, D 2010, 'Consolidation in a wildlife tourism

industry: the changing impact of whale shark tourist expenditure in the Ningaloo Coast Region', *International Journal of Tourism Research* 12: 134-148

Catalyst 2007, Whale sharks transcript, November, www.abc.net.au/catalyst/stories/s2084913.htm.

Holmberg, J, Norman, B & Arzoumanian, Z 2009, 'Estimating population size, structure, and residency time for whale sharks Rhincodon typus through collaborative photo-identification', *Endangered Species Research* 7: 39-53.

Ecocean 2012, accessed April 24, 2012, www.whaleshark.org.

Ecocean 2011, Ecocean whaleshark photo ID library, accessed September 1, 2011, www.whaleshark.org.

Java.com 2005, Duke's Choice Awards winners: Ecocean whale shark photo identification library, accessed November 2007, http://java.com/en/desktop/ecocean.jsp.

Norman, B & Stevens, J 2007, 'Size and maturity status of the whale shark (Rhincodon typus) at Ningaloo Reef in Western Australia', *Fisheries Research* 84: 81-86.

Rolex Awards 2006, Photography fingerprints the biggest fish. Developing an effective system of identification to protect the whale shark, accessed November 2007, www.rolexawards.com/laureates/laureate-86-norman.html.

Whale Shark and Oceanic Research Centre 2010, Conservation, accessed September 1, 2011, www.wsorc.org/index.php?p=Conservation.

Chapter 4

Xanterra LLC

Networking for the[ir] future

JACK CARLSEN AND DEBORAH EDWARDS

INTRODUCTION

In many sectors of the economy, there has been an evolution in management practices towards more sustainable modes of operation. This has involved all facets of business operation, from procurement and production through to marketing, sales, packaging and labeling. Climate change and cognisance of the greenhouse emissions generated in the process of production of goods and services will keep the focus on the environmental performance of businesses and government well into the future (Carlsen & Callender 2009). Procurement is positioned as the starting point for improved environmental performance and transition towards more economically viable, socially acceptable and environmentally sustainable business practices. Thus, it is an essential component of the environmental performance and sustainability of many tourism firms. Increasingly, innovation in supply chain management is becoming a focus of many tourism operations, so much so that some companies now have dedicated Environmental Management Strategies (EMS) divisions, reporting processes and auditing programs built in to their organisational structure.

This case study presents the EMS and environmentally-focused procurement policy of America's (and possibly the world's) largest nature-based tourism operation, Xanterra LLC. Xanterra is the United States of America's largest national park concessionaire, operating tourism businesses in 24 locations (Table 4.1) that received 18 million visitors, including 1.9 million overnight visitors, in 2010. A concessionaire is a firm that operates a business belonging to another entity under a concession, usually as the only seller of certain goods or services. A concessionaire pays either a fixed sum or a percentage of revenue to the entity with the ability to assign exclusive rights for an area or facility.

Table 4.1 Xanterra LLC parks and resorts 2010

Parks and resorts	
Petrified Forest National Park	Burr Oak State Park
Yellowstone National Park	Furnace Creek Inn & Ranch
Deer Creek State Park	Geneva Marina
Rocky Mountain National Park	Gideon Putnam Resort
Bryce Canyon National Park	Grand Canyon Railway
Mount Rushmore National Memorial	Hueston Woods State Park
Crater Lake National Park	Maumee Bay State Park
Kingsmill Resort	Mohican State Park
Everglades National Park	Punderson Manor State Park
Zion National Park	Salt Fork State Park

Xanterra's concession operations include hotels, lodges, restaurants, retail, campgrounds, transportation systems, buses, shuttles, snow coaches, snowmobiles and boats. Behind the scenes, they operate vehicle maintenance facilities, building maintenance facilities, paint shops, carpentry shops, print shops, upholstery shops, kitchens, warehouses, fleet vehicles, employee dormitories and facilities, and administrative facilities. In Yellowstone National Park alone they have over 900 buildings.

Xanterra's Environmental Management System (EMS), Ecologix, is the source of a range of innovations that are the focus of this case study. Ecologix is a logical integration of ecology and business. According to Gina McIlwraith, Environment, Health and Safety Director, Ecologix ensures:

- continual improvement of their environmental performance;
- compliance with all environmental regulations;
- incorporation of best management practices; and
- flexibility to respond to property environmental priorities.

Drivers of innovation

The most succinct reason for pursuing innovation in all of Xanterra's operations through the Ecologix EMS is captured in Xanterra's Mission Statement, as follows:

> Xanterra's mission is to be the industry leader in park and resort hospitality. We are committed to practicing integrity and quality, maintaining positive relationships with our employees and clients, leading in environmental stewardship and creating unforgettable memories for our guests.

Our business decisions balance economic viability with ecological responsibility.

We reduce and recycle waste, conserve energy and water, and educate our guests and employees on environmental stewardship.

We believe that increasing the sustainability of natural systems is not just good business. It is the right thing to do.

There is a belief within the organisation that sustaining natural systems through continuous innovation and improvement is not only good for the environments in which they operate, but also good business. Employees are asked to hold management to account for all operational decisions that relate to environmental performance. Thus, they have both a top-down mission and a bottom-up monitoring mechanism to ensure continuous improvement in environmental performance, compliance with environmental regulations and responsiveness to environmental priorities.

Barriers to innovation

Introduction of Xanterra's innovative EMS system Ecologix was an extensive and costly exercise for the organisation, posing a significant internal barrier. It also remains to be seen whether the system will translate into actual improvements in environmental performance. Hence, it is both costly and risky. However, by monitoring progress towards measurable and achievable goals on an annual basis as it moves towards its 2015 targets, using the year 2000 as a baseline, it is able to report improved environmental performance across all areas of Xanterra's operations, including energy efficiency, diversion of waste and sustainable cuisine purchases.

The ISO 14001 standard upon which it is based is not prescriptive. ISO is a basic process framework, initially intended for the manufacturing/industrial sector. While it requires an EMS, regular audits and commitment to continuous improvement, it does not require environmental performance levels to be met. It is one thing to have an EMS in place (on the shelf) but it is another thing to actually achieve changes, such as reductions in resource consumption. The effectiveness of ISO depends upon the will and intention of each company employing it.

Therefore, Xanterra had to, first of all, gain top management support for the EMS program and then set about designing and implementing the program with the support of all staff members. The whole process was scrutinised by public and private agencies with an interest in US parks. The process has also taken place within a highly competitive environment for concession contracts in US parks. Concessionaires not only have to compete on cost, but must also demonstrate strong environmental performance. It has been far from easy, but Xanterra has made significant innovations in all aspects of their business and environmental performance and procurement.

Processes for innovation

Xanterra's Ecologix EMS involves a continuous improvement process, based on achieving a truly sustainable business by the year 2015 with the following characteristics:

- using zero fossil fuels;
- using zero persistent toxic chemicals;
- generating zero landfill waste;
- consuming water only to the extent that no species are negatively affected;
- employing sustainable design, construction and maintenance practices in all operations;
- serving 100 percent local organic food;
- selling 100 percent fair trade products; and
- not affecting flora or fauna species through development.

In order to achieve this, they have set the following ten-year targets for all areas of operation:

- *Transportation:* Achieve company-wide CAFÉ standard of 35 mpg (EPA rated combined city/highway mileage) for all vehicles purchased by 2015.
- *Emissions:* Decrease greenhouse gas (CO_2) emissions by 30 percent (baseline year 2000).
- *Solid Waste:* Divert from landfill 50 percent of all solid waste generated.
- *Hazardous Waste:* Generate zero hazardous waste.
- *Water:* Decrease water usage by 25 percent (baseline year 2000).
- *Energy:* Decrease fossil fuel usage by 30 percent (baseline year 2000); increase renewable energy to 7 percent of total electricity usage.
- *Food:* Purchase of sustainable food items to 50 percent of all companywide food expenditure.

Ecologix is described as a hybrid EMS, as it includes aspects of compliance, sustainability and accountability. It is based on the ISO 14001 Certification and the National Environment Performance Track [NEPT] programs and began with top management setting an environmental policy expressing commitment to compliance and continual improvement.

Planning for Ecologix was undertaken by forming a cross-functional team to complete a comprehensive review of a facility's environmental activities that have potential to interact with the environment. Significant environmental aspects were addressed by setting objectives and measurable targets which include activities such as controlling the aspect (e.g. inspecting a chemical storage area to ensure zero spills) and continuous improvement (e.g. reducing energy use by 10 percent each year).

Thus, Xanterra has a management structure that incorporates these objectives and targets into its programs and procedures. These translate into work instructions to train employees in the EMS and ensure competence to carry out their responsibilities. In terms of monitoring, everything is documented so that progress towards goals is continually checked and corrective action is taken when necessary. There are procedures for monitoring and measuring activities and for handling non-conformance. Periodic auditing and annual management review of the efficacy of the whole system is completed.

Networks for innovation

Xanterra procures almost $40 million of foodstuffs annually to meet the needs of its guests (Table 4.2). Thus, in addition to the certification and external collaborations that support innovation, Xanterra has engaged their extensive procurement and supplier organisations in the process of improving environmental performance.

Table 4.2 Xanterra LLC annual food procurement

Value (US$)	Quantities
$30m of food	250,000 lbs of fish
$1m of vehicles	16,000 gallons of ketchup
$1m of chemicals	110,000 gallons of ice cream
$1m of seafood	380,000 rolls of toilet paper
$2m of produce	380,000 lbs of french fries
$3.5m of meat	32,000 cases soda
$500,000 of sheets/towels	65,000 gallons of fountain syrup
	70,000 lbs of coffee
	4.5m hot and cold cups

By introducing an innovative, environmentally-focused procurement policy, Xanterra has been able to develop:

- an environmentally preferred procurement (EPP) policy with quantifiable goals and targets;
- a formal assessment protocol to determine if a product or service is environmentally preferable;
- an inventory of environmentally preferable products;
- an environmentally preferable capital expenditures protocol to assist in weighing the attributes and impacts of capital items prior to purchase;
- a letter to contractors explaining environmental goals and contractor responsibilities;
- a letter to vendors and a policy on product packaging that explains environmental goals and vendor responsibilities;

- a guide for properties on how to purchase fuel-efficient vehicles;
- a sustainable cuisine program to purchase more organic, local, sustainable food products; and
- a formal company-wide policy banning certain species of fish from menus and recommending others.

Xanterra applies its EPP to all products and all areas of operation by guiding staff members in making purchases that use less energy, cost less to transport, generate less waste, are more recyclable, are more durable, require less packaging and are less toxic without compromising service quality. Every item, from office supplies to food and beverages, cleaning products to new buildings, is subject to a formal process to determine whether items meet stringent EPP criteria based on US Environmental Protection Agency (EPA) standards. Xanterra South Rim has a Green Purchasing Gold Achievement Award from the US EPA for its use of items with a recycled content including paper, clothing and plastic. Use of recycled materials also saved the company $55,000 in disposal costs in 2005.

Xanterra's sustainable cuisine program promotes foods that are produced, processed, packaged and delivered with minimum impact on the environment. The program requires food and beverage managers, chefs and purchasing agents to consider the procurement of organic and locally produced foods. These foods are now a growing part of sustainable cuisine purchase, with their value increasing from $1.4 million in 2004 to $5.7 million in 2009, totaling 19.6 per cent across all food purchases. Sustainable products include beer and wine, seafood, tea and coffee, meat and dairy products. Punderson Manor State Park and Mount Rushmore are locations that are now providing quality organic produce from onsite garden operations.

Accommodation buildings represent the core business activity of Xanterra and consequently account for most of the environmental impacts, including:

- 65 percent of total electricity consumption;
- 30 percent of total greenhouse gas emissions;
- 136 million tons of construction, demolition and land clearing (CDL) waste (approx. 2.8 lbs/person/day); and
- 12 percent of potable water use.

Xanterra's Guidelines for Environmentally Sustainable Design define Xanterra's expectations for all contractors, subcontractors, architects, engineers, consultants and vendors working with Xanterra on the design, construction, or rehabilitation of buildings in national parks. Through an extensive program of retrofitting and replacement in the areas of waste management, energy, building and transportation, considerable reductions in the energy footprint have been achieved. In particular, buildings which account for the highest energy and resource use and generate the most solid, liquid and gaseous waste have been the focus of the Ecologix program. New designs and technologies have been incorporated into all 'green' buildings and suites, producing the following benefits:

- ecological benefits;
- decreased operating costs;
- increased worker productivity;
- raising the bar for market competitors;
- shorter return on investment (RoI) periods;
- recognition by US GBC and local media; and
- becoming the industry standard and guide for environmentally sustainable design and construction.

Xanterra now has 23 corporate environmental policies as part of Ecologix. To accomplish their goals, they work collaboratively with a number of government, corporate and non-profit organisations to build effective and efficient partnerships. Active alliances with the stakeholders are assisting Xanterra to move closer to realizing its goal of sustainability.

Summary

Introduction of Xanterra's innovative EMS system, Ecologix, was an extensive and costly exercise for the organisation. It also remains to be seen as to what will translate into actual improvements in environmental performance. Not only was it costly, but it may also prove to be risky. However, by monitoring progress towards measurable and achievable goals on an annual basis as it moves towards its 2015 targets, using the year 2000 as a baseline, Xanterra is able to report improved environmental performance across all areas of its operations, including energy efficiency, diversion of waste and sustainable cuisine purchases.

Xanterra's EMS and environmentally preferred procurement programs have yielded significant benefits for the company, its employees and customers and the environment in which it operates. For a company that operates in some of America's most iconic and fragile environments, the need for environmental integrity is critical, not only for economic, but also for ecological reasons. Above all, Xanterra believes that balancing economic viability with ecological responsibility is not only good business, but also the ethical thing to do.

The environmentally preferred procurement program is a cornerstone of Xanterra's corporate mission and vision and has been embraced by all employees within the organisation. They have set ambitious and measurable 2015 targets for environmental performance, have implemented the program across all areas of operations and monitor and report their progress annually to all employees, suppliers and customers. This has positioned the company in a place of leadership in environmental compliance, and provided a distinct competitive advantage in operating concessions in US national and state parks. It has also proved to be a good business strategy, as it has reduced costs and liabilities in the short term and may lead to increased profitability in the longer term. In 2008, Xanterra LLC was purchased by American billionaire Phil Anschutz, but the change of ownership did not affect the organisation at the level of management and all environmental programs were maintained (Whitehust 2008).

References

Carlsen, J 2008, *From Green Procurement to Sustainable Procurement: The Case of Xanterra L.L.C. In: Building Practice and Research Collaboration*, Proceedings of the 17th International Purchasing and Supply Education and Research Association Conference, Curtin University, Perth, WA: 349-354.

Carlsen, J & Callender, G 2009, 'Sustainable Procurement – A Guide for Research and Practice', in *Proceedings of the 18th IPSERA Conference*, European Business School, Oestrich Winkel, Germany: 904-934.

Carlsen, J & Edwards, D 2008, 'BEST EN case studies: Innovation for sustainable tourism', *Tourism and Hospitality Research* 8(1): 44-55.

Whitehurst, P 2008, 'New Ownership for Xanterra, GC Railway', *Williams News*, 26 June.

Xanterra, accessed 11 April 2012, www.xanterra.com/Environmental-Action-364.html.

Chapter 5

The Diablo Trust
Planning sustainable land use

JACK CARLSEN AND DEBORAH EDWARDS

INTRODUCTION

In 1993, two Arizona ranch families, the Prossers of the Bar T Bar Ranch and the Metzgers of the Flying M Ranch, both located in Northern Arizona, initiated a land stewardship collaboration called the Diablo Trust. The idea was to develop a collaborative process that included the wide and disparate views and agendas from ranchers, state and federal agencies, wildlife enthusiasts, academics and environmentalists.

The Trust was named after the Diablo Canyon that separates the two ranches, and was formed to promote the social, biological and economic sustainability of federal, state and private lands by engaging in a collaborative stewardship process in harmony with the natural environment and broader community. Their mission is to ensure the long-term economic, social and ecological sustainability of the Diablo Trust land area by providing a forum for active community participation in a collaborative land stewardship process.

Diablo Trust is an open organisation in which participation is free. Funds are raised through donations, fundraising events, and grants for operations and special projects. Volunteers provide labour for events and land projects. Participants of the Trust are diverse and include, *inter alia*, ranchers, environmentalists, land managers, government agencies, scientists, researchers, non-owner land and resource agencies, institutions, teachers, students, artists and formal groups. Their goal is to demonstrate innovative approaches to restore and maintain the natural processes that create and protect a healthy, unfragmented landscape to support a diverse flourishing community of human, plant and animal life in the Diablo Trust land area. Related to this are the following sub-goals:

- sustaining open space (preventing land fragmentation);
- sustaining biological diversity;
- sustaining multiple-generation stewards working on the land;
- producing high-quality food;
- protecting watersheds with stable living soils;
- restoring historic grasslands;
- enhancing wildlife corridors; and
- achieving community of place.

The Trust undertakes a range of projects designed to enhance collaboration and learning about the land and the effects of management, recreation, climate, fire and time. Projects have included science and monitoring, artists' days, educational outreach, wildlife protection, community outreach, educational programs for local schools, ranch management, and land and watershed improvements.

The Diablo Canyon Rural Planning Area project arose out of an innovative approach to rural planning in Arizona between 1998 and 2000, called the 'Growing Smarter Legislation'. Landowners were encouraged to petition for the establishment of land trusts that would effectively assume planning responsibility for rural farming lands and adjacent tenures within Arizona. A planning meeting held at the Flying M Ranch in the autumn of 2003 led to the formation of the Diablo Canyon Rural Planning Area (RPA). It was the first trust of its kind in Northern Arizona and effectively transferred control of the planning and permitting process for the Diablo Canyon Area to the Diablo Trust.

According to its Vision Statement, the Diablo Canyon RPA serves as a model approach for the continuation of traditional working ranches as long-term, economically-viable enterprises while maintaining unfragmented landscapes and restoring native ecosystems. The RPA successfully integrates economy, ecology, and community by pursuing a range of economic opportunities necessary to support and maintain the viability of ranching while recognizing the fundamental importance of the health of the land and the support of the broader community.

Drivers of innovation

The key driver for the formation of the Diablo Canyon RPA was the increasing pressure on the historic uses of century-old homesteads and the ranches associated with them. The Prossers and Metzgers feared that the traditional cattle ranches and the families that run them would not survive. They aimed to protect traditional agriculture by preserving farmlands and developing options for value-adding products, tourism and alternative land uses. The two families both recognised the need to join forces to preserve their land and the traditions connected to it that were under increasing environmental and economic pressures.

They also recognised the need to communicate with the local community and conservation groups regarding their efforts to preserve grasslands, not only for cattle, but also for the wildlife that inhabits the area. Antelope, pronghorn, elk and deer cohabit with cattle on their properties, and they have made considerable effort to protect wildlife habitat by working with the National Resource Conservation Service. Besides practical measures such as fencing cattle out of wetlands and using rest-rotation grazing during drought periods, they have also taken innovative steps to aid wildlife through the provision of water sources and monitoring of wildlife populations.

Finally, there was a desire to pass on a viable business operation to future generations of family ranchers, which in itself is a key dimension of economic, cultural and social sustainability. The cyclical nature of ranching operations and the high cost of improvements combined with the pressure to make public land available for residential development drove the desire to create alternative economic opportunities to supplement ranch operations.

Barriers to innovation

There were many internal barriers for these farming families, not the least of which was the global trend toward intensive farming of beef in feedlots leading to the failure of traditional farming methods such as cattle ranching. Another less tangible internal barrier was the capacity of the members of the Diablo Trust who imagined that 'they could do anything' on their lands, which turned out not to be the case. Whilst a number of options were identified in the RPA, they each present their own challenges and barriers that limit their economic viability and/or cultural desirability. These will be discussed below.

The production of high-quality, natural or organic beef for niche markets had been done in other parts of the American West, and three examples — Babbitt Ranches, Oregon Country Beef and Ervin's Natural Beef — were cited. Key questions centred on whether to provide the beef product in fresh or frozen form and the viability of accessing meat processing facilities. Getting these products into production and then to market would require considerable investment in infrastructure and distribution systems: this presented a major financial external barrier.

Tourism, recreation and education also presented many internal and external barriers. Hosting visitors would require a huge effort by the ranchers, who are already busy with their activities. Other on-farm activities involving recreation and education programs were also considered, but their small scale meant that they may not be commercially viable. The cost associated with public liability insurance is also a major barrier to entry into this form of tourism, especially if an authentic experience of ranching and all of the hazards associated with it are to be offered. Finally, the presentation and communication skills of the local workers who could work in tourism may also be a constraint to the success of any tourism ventures.

Wood product production was considered as an innovation that would address two issues. Firstly, it would reduce the area of juniper and pinyon trees, making more land available for grazing. Juniper was an invasive species that was destroying grasslands and a program of reduction was already in place. Secondly, it would provide a source of commercial firewood production to meet demand in the cold Northern Arizona winters. However, tree-clearing and firewood collection are highly labour intensive and there are many other sources of fuel for home log-fires, including packaged, manufactured logs with guaranteed three-hour burn times and even with crackling that imitates the sound of real, burning wood!

Commercial banks of wind turbines that generate power for the grid can be found on many farming lands, and the rent that these sites generate for land owners is substantial. However, they have a tendency to ruin the rural vistas and aesthetics, and as such meet with considerable resistance whenever they are proposed in open landscapes. View sheds in Northern Arizona can extend for 60 miles (100 kilometres) or more and in themselves provide a great sense of space for the millions of tourists that view the area on the way to world-class attractions such as the Grand Canyon and Monument Valley. Locating wind turbines on farms requires consideration not only of engineering factors such as proximity to the grid, but also of aesthetic considerations (effects on vistas and view sheds) and any impact on wildlife habitat and birdlife.

Finally, housing development presents perhaps the biggest issue for farmers, as land sold off for housing will be lost to farming forever. All farmers, no matter where they live, want to retain or indeed expand their land holdings in order to attain economies of scale and more economically viable farm production. Partial sale of farmlands would, however, enable farmers to keep their ranch houses and the majority of their lands, so a careful plan for developing land has to be put in place.

Processes for innovation

There were two steps involved in this innovative approach to saving and sustaining land and traditions in the area. First was establishing the Diablo Trust as the entity that would assume planning responsibility for the area. This was undertaken by the Metzger and Prosser families, owners of the two long-time ranches in the area, the Flying M and the Bar T Bar ranches. They began a process of petitioning the County Board for approval to form a rural planning area.

The second step was to develop the Diablo Regional Planning Area (DRPA) that would guide new economic development opportunities within this area of approximately 20 by 40 miles (426,000 acres). The area was a 'checkerboard' of different land uses and private, state and federal tenures, and ranged from forests to high desert country (see Figure 6.1).

This area in northeast Arizona is the heartlands of the American West, characterised by the ranchers and cowboys that were the stuff of legends and the source of images portrayed through books and movies of the 'wild west'. Now, there are many competing land uses and the process of planning and managing the land involves many stakeholders, as well as integration with the County Comprehensive Plan. There was a need to educate the public about the importance of public land ranching and the environmental stewardship practices that ranchers had in place. A weekend workshop was the venue for the ranches to recruit new members to the trust, such as the Sierra Club, which was not aware of the Ranchers' efforts with regard to land management and preservation.

Figure 6.1 The Diablo Canyon planning area

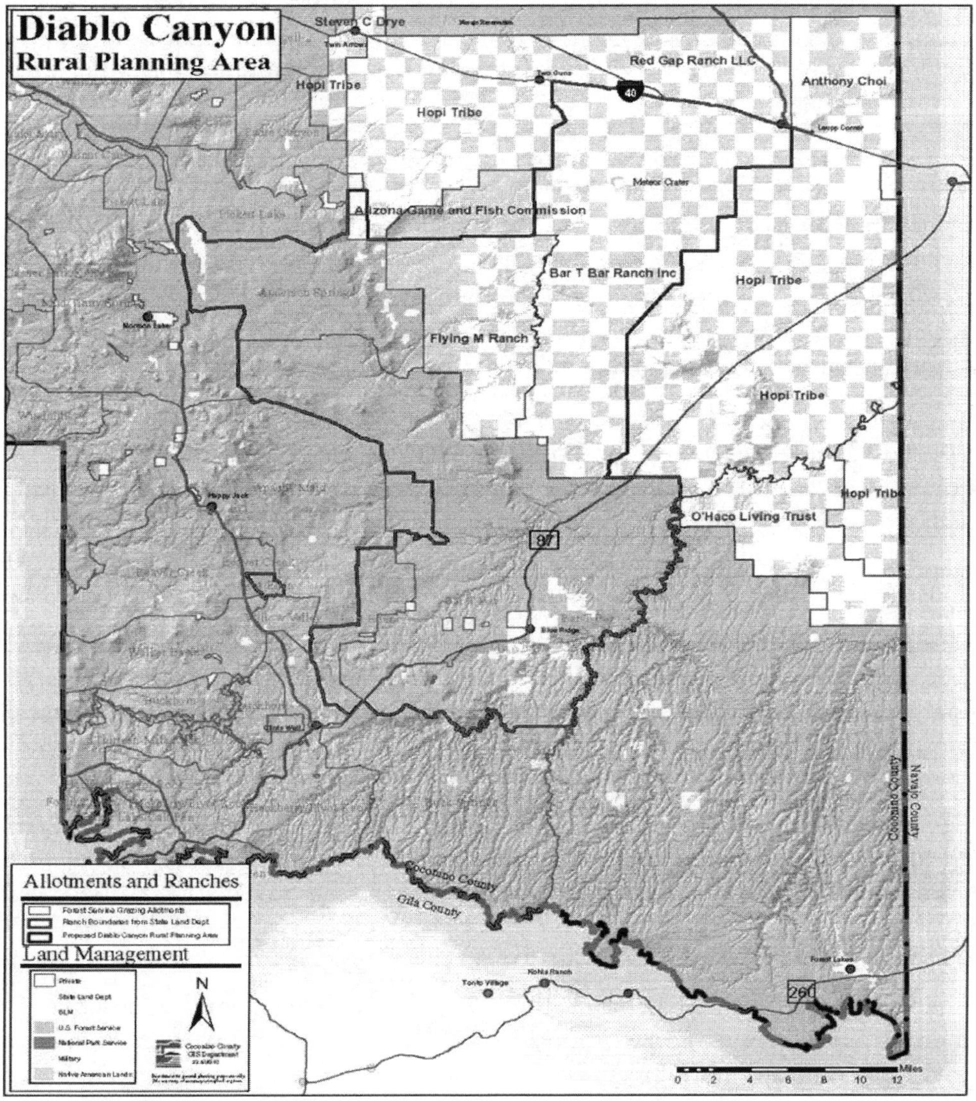

Source: www.diablotrust.org/about_where.htm (accessed 31 March 2008).

With regard to commercial operations, all land use options identified in the plan, although tried before in other parts of the West with limited success, were considered worthy for inclusion. These options were all commercially focused, although some also had environmental benefits, and included:

- value-added beef;
- tourism, recreation and education;
- wood products;
- energy development; and
- housing.

Value-added beef would be a niche-market product for consumers seeking more natural grass-fed and organic meat products. Products could be sold locally through direct marketing at farmers markets, community-supported agriculture (see also Chapter 5), food co-operatives/clubs, local restaurants and other more flexible arrangements, such as on-site sales.

Tourism, recreation and education opportunities were also considered to share a great experience of life in the West on a working cattle ranch. Activities could include horse riding, guided tours, lodging, themed festivals and special events and facilities could include cultural centers, educational museums, historical museums, shooting ranges and off-road vehicle facilities. The ranches are located close to the famous Route 66 and the Grand Canyon, areas that are rich in Native American culture and natural history and attract millions of visitors annually.

Wood production had been a minor part of ranch operations and was largely a by-product of grassland restoration and clearing of pinyon and juniper trees. Commercial wood-products could include those that require minimal processing, such as firewood and roundwood, to manufactured wood products such as fireplace logs, lumber, laminated beams made from Ponderosa Pine and composite materials. Again, the need for coordinated supply and a production facility were recognised in the RPA before any commercial wood production could take place on ranches.

Energy development in the form of alternative energy sources has been driven by rising fossil fuel costs and the associated environmental consequences. Regulations of the power generation industry and state tax incentives have focused attention on two alternative energy options in Arizona: biomass and wind. Wind mapping has taken place on both ranches, and meteorological 'test' towers have improved the viability of a number of sites. Wind energy production provides an opportunity for ranchers to generate lease and royalty incomes and avoid sale or sub-division of ranchlands.

Finally, housing development is the most common economic alternative for ranchers in Arizona, with subdivision into 40-acre land parcels known as ranchettes resulting in fragmentation of wildlife habitats and loss of open spaces. Notwithstanding the undesirability of housing in the RPA, there is provision for a form of 'protected development' where a limited amount of land can be sold off while still preserving the integrity of the ranchlands.

Details of each of these options are cited in the RPA and include fresh or frozen beef products, 'dude ranches' and other ecotourism, recreation and education opportunities, firewood products, wind power generation and housing development. It is important to recognise that all of these options will impact on the sustainability of the ranch operations and may or may not be compatible with sustainable tourism development.

Networks for innovation

The Diablo Trust arose for a single purpose — to protect traditional farming families — so it was not really involved with other groups. In fact, it was described as an 'accidental organisation' that had to embrace all land management issues in the area, taking it well beyond its original task. Having established the Trust, the members then began the process of engagement with other groups such as tourism bodies, whom they originally viewed with caution. Developers, too, were viewed with suspicion, but bringing these groups together around the table was critical to developing the regional plan. Rather than 'dining with the devil', this engagement with all other land users was considered as 'embracing thine enemy' and openly considering all options for protecting and preserving the farming lands. The Metzger and Prosser family members of the Trust believe that this engagement with land developers is one of the most constructive outcomes of the planning process.

Pursuing the economic opportunities identified in the RPA would also require engagement with production and marketing agencies. Beef production would require access to approved production facilities and direct-marketing channels in order to get a high-quality product to consumers. Tourism, recreation and education would require engagement with tourism authorities and business consultants that have expertise in the business of ecotourism and cultural tourism. Wood production and wind energy would require considerable investment by public and private entities, as would housing development.

Maintaining relationship and knowledge continuity with agencies and networks when key people retire or move away is significant to successful innovative collaboration. To maintain the momentum in their relationships with other agencies, the Diablo Trust created a 'transition document'. The aim of the document is to assist new agency staff and members of the Diablo Trust collaborative in understanding Diablo Trust's mission statement, purpose, goals, organisational history and structure, board members and staff and key strategies the collaborative uses to meet goals.

Knowledge continuity is being achieved through the Collaborative Resource Operational Plan (CROP), designed to address agency turnover and discontinuity. CROP is a database that contains maps and documents the history of current and completed projects on the Diablo Trust land area including brush management, water improvements, prescribed burns and facilities implementation. The aim of the CROP database is to help facilitate the transition of incoming and outgoing agency personnel who work closely with the Diablo Trust. The plan includes input from state and federal agency representatives, ranchers and the Diablo Trust.

In recognition of their efforts, the Diablo Trust was honored with the BEEF 2011 Trailblazer Award. The annual award is presented to a producer or group of producers whose farsighted leadership and efforts help promote or realise significant research, programs or actions that benefit and improve the production and profit environment for US beef producers.

Summary

Innovation can be both necessary and practical and will not always require extensive research and new technology, especially when it comes to dealing with the universal problems of rural land management. However, this case study indicates that relationships and collaborative alliances are critical to solving problems and driving and maintaining innovation. By working with local, state and federal agencies, community and conservation groups, educational institutions and each other, these two long-time farming families took considerable steps to improve land management practices, conserve habitat for wildlife, maintain their farming traditions and ensure that the land remains representative of all of the values associated with the American West.

References

Carlsen, J & Edwards, D 2008, 'BEST EN case studies: Innovation for sustainable tourism', *Tourism and Hospitality Research* 8(1): 44-55.

Diablo Trust, accessed 30 March 2012, www.diablotrust.org/index.htm.

Diablo Trust, Timeline, accessed 2 March 2012, www.diablotrust.org/docs/dt.accomplishments.2011.pdf.

Chapter 6

Tasting Arizona
Sustainable Food Networks

Jack Carlsen and Deborah Edwards

INTRODUCTION

Tasting Arizona is a network of tourism, non-government, indigenous, farming, education, community, festival and food organisations that aims to provide 'local flavour' to customers in Arizona. The consortium believes that consumers want local flavour, and has identified a range of food products that represent the taste and feel of Arizona. Tasting Arizona represents an innovative approach to reviving local foods and traditional farming activities and countering the decline in small farming communities taking place in the US.

The benefits of this revival extend well beyond providing visitors with local flavours, as the foods are linked with preserving traditional farming practices, conserving areas for wildlife, educating youth, keeping food pure and free from genetic modification, maintaining agricultural diversity and biodiversity and protecting cultural traditions. Wild foods such as the mesquite bean flour and pure varieties of fruit and vegetables are just two examples of traditional local foods that have been revived.

Tasting Arizona began as a series of workshops held by the Center for Sustainable Environments (CSE) at Northern Arizona University (NAU). CSE was a university-based sustainability science group with a focus on reducing the impacts of food production, transport and processing on biodiversity, food security, and water and energy consumption. CSE undertook educational, research and outreach activities in partnership with university, non-profit, federal and community groups (see Tables 6.1 and 6.2) with the aim of adopting more sustainable practices.

Table 6.1 Center for Sustainable Environments collaborators

University	Community	Federal	Community
Bilby Research Centre	Environmental Leadership through Mentoring	Colorado Plate Cooperative Ecosystems Studies Unit	Diablo Trust (see also Chapter 6)
Centennial Forest	Grand Canyon Trust	Environmental Protection Authority	Slow Food USA
Center for Environmental Sciences and Education	Grand Canyon Wild Lands Council	Environmental Technology Consortium	Trust for Public Land
Earthnotes on KNAU - Public Radio	Indigenous Community Enterprises	National Park Service	Friends of Flagstaff's Future
Ecological Restoration institute	Second Nature	Southwest Biological Science Center/Colorado Plate Field Station	Greater Flagstaff Forest Partnership
Environmental	Terralingua: Partnerships in Linguistic and Biological Diversity		
Forest ERA	Wild Farm Alliance		
Institute for Tribal Environmental Professionals			
Land-use history of Colorado Plate			
Master of Liberal Studies: Good and Sustainable Communities			
Merriam-Powell Center for Environmental Research			
Navajo Nation Archaeology Department at NAU			

University	Community	Federal	Community
Program in Community Culture and Environment			
Quaternary Sciences at NAU			
Watershed Research and Education Program			

Source: http://home.nau.edu/environment/default.asp (accessed 31 March 2008).

Table 6.2 Partners in Tasting Arizona

Tourism providers	Local growers (farmers and ranchers)
Farmers markets	Foragers of wild foods
Non-profit organisations	Restaurants
Tribes	Food enthusiasts
Schools	University researchers
Hospitals	Plant and seed sellers
National and State Parks (Slide Rock)	Heritage food growers
Festival organisers	Youth gardens
Community Supported Agriculture [CSA]	Community gardens

A joint project of the CSE and the Leopold Centre for Sustainable Agriculture of Iowa State University identified emerging opportunities for Arizona's farmers, ranchers, orchardists, foragers and retailers to benefit from the growing interest in place-based heritage foods of Arizona. They found that Arizona is well placed to promote natural and cultural heritage foods, sustainable production, biodiversity and novel nutritional foods through the agricultural and ecotourism networks of Arizona. Furthermore, they have, through a statewide poll, identified a high demand for heritage foods, especially amongst the Native American communities that are preventing nutrition-related diseases such as diabetes and heart disease using heritage foods. Thus, heritage foods could provide a range of economic, ecological, cultural and social benefits for the communities of Arizona that have the willingness and knowledge to support place-based heritage food production (Nabhan, West & Pirog 2005).

Drivers of innovation

The food systems of the Canyon Country, also known as the Colorado Plateau or Four Corners Region, are amongst the oldest and most culturally diverse in North America. Although the state of Arizona celebrated its centenary in 2012, traditional agriculture in the form of corn and squash cultivation had been in practice in Tucson, Arizona some 4,100 years. Also, some of the oldest breeds of sheep (the Navajo Churro) and cattle (the Corriente of Spanish Criollo ancestry) persist in Canyon Country. Prior to agriculture, wild foraging for the pinion nuts, greens, acorns and fruits that are native to the area had been going on for over 10,000 years. It is these wild and traditional food systems that have been recognised and revitalised as heritage foods, offering Arizonans and visitors a 'taste of the landscape'.

Tasting Arizona believed that heritage foods are good for everybody: producers, consumers and visitors. In addition to the community benefits, there are indications that wild foods have previously unknown health benefits in preventing blood sugar and insulin sensitivity and curbing adult-onset diabetes and obesity. Certain foods such as white corn are central to traditional cultural ceremonies, yet these pure varieties are under threat from cross-pollination with genetically modified varieties of corn.

Increased recognition and concern about greenhouse gas emissions, global warming, environmental degradation and the use of fossil fuels in food production have been captured in the concept of food miles. Food miles refer to the distance food travels from the place of production to the place of final consumption, which in the US is estimated at 1,500 miles. Consuming locally grown food not only supports local farming communities but also reduces the carbon footprint of food production, as well as reducing the cost of transportation, thereby addressing the broader issues of social, environmental and economic sustainability.

Food production and distribution can take place in urban as well as rural areas, with farmers markets, harvest festivals and youth gardens providing venues where food producers and consumers can meet. Farmers markets are flourishing in the US, where there are over 3,500 operating nationwide. Harvest festivals not only celebrate the farming traditions of rural areas, but also act as a catalyst for tourism and community celebration. Involving youth in community food gardens is also a good way to revitalise interest and demand for fresh, local foods and has the added social benefit of increasing interaction between youth and elders in the community. These initiatives have not only increased the quantity of local food produced and consumed, but also the variety of food. They have also re-connected food with the seasons and sense of place in which it is produced.

Hence, the drivers of innovation for Tasting Arizona relate to the growing cultural and ecological awareness of people and partner agencies within the Colorado Plateau and federally across the United States (US) about the importance of maintaining the health, security and sustainability of food systems and local communities. Ultimately, the customer is the driver of demand for local produce and there is a range of initiatives in place in order to both grow and meet that growing demand.

Barriers to innovation

The challenges are many: as natural and farming lands are under increasing pressure from larger producers, customers have become used to buying out-of-season and non-local produce, and the distribution system does not favor small producers. In addition to these external market barriers, there are the internal limitations of the scale of production that prevent traditional and wild food producers from achieving continuity of supply. Small farmers are also subject to seasonal variations and are under threat from fire and drought, which could wipe out a season's production. Most farmers, ranchers and producers do not use pesticides, herbicides or chemicals, so their crops are more exposed to plant disease and insect infestation.

Family farms and ranches are rapidly declining as urban expansion and large-scale farming takes place across rural areas of the US. Locally produced food has been declining as water has been diverted for other economic activities. There is also a lack of place-based agriculture and agricultural diversity as the trend to source mass-produced foods from outside of the local area continues.

Processes for innovation

The first step in reviving the traditional and wild foods was to create a food network to maintain and strengthen local food systems. Community-supported agriculture (CSA) programs provide a means for residents to make a commitment to support local agriculture and share the inherent risks and benefits of seasonal farming. CSA models are flexible and can be run as non-profit organisations, voluntary groups or by farmers themselves. The Flagstaff CSA was established by Crooked Sky Farms in 2002 in partnership with 70 members and has grown to over 290 members since. It operates three twelve-week seasons in fall, winter and spring, with a break in the summer season so that members can support the Flagstaff Community Farmers Market. Each member becomes a shareholder in a season of production, on the understanding that there are neither refunds nor guarantees of a specific amount of produce. Each share provides for vegetables on a weekly basis that must be picked up from the Bilby Research Center at NAU. Information on other local products is also made available to CSA members. In this way, the CSA is creating a sustainable food system, supporting the local economy and fostering stewardship and connection with the land.

Bringing back local farmers markets provides a place for celebration of local foods and interaction between producers, restaurants and consumers. Supporting local farms involves identifying traditional food varieties, orchard restoration, sponsorship of festivals and food events, inviting chefs to prepare local produce and creating food and wine trails. Helping visitors to discover local foods in this way will increase demand and encourage more producers to get involved.

Engaging with youth in creating and farming community gardens that have local varieties is also effective in both increasing demand and strengthening supply. In addition, introducing wild foods to visitors and residents in familiar ways, such as cookies made from mesquite flour, which is naturally sweet, has proven successful. Wild food walks provide opportunities for linking wild foods to wildlife and preserving natural areas. Declaration of themed National Heritage Areas provides an opportunity to access one million dollars per year in funding for the development of tours and the production of maps of farming and wild food areas in Arizona and neighbouring states. In this way, tourists can be engaged in discovering new foods and supporting local producers.

One of the more innovative programs is the preservation of heirloom apple orchards adjacent to the Slide Rock State Parks, in the popular tourism destination of Sedona. Only four of the ten varieties of apples first planted in 1912 remain in the orchard, and none of these are available commercially. In partnership with State Parks and NAU, the historic fruit and nut orchards are being mapped and restored through a process of replanting and water system evaluations that should protect the orchards against the further ravages of fire, drought and time.

The process of engagement of residents and visitors in the revival of local food networks is taking place through a variety of small-scale initiatives. Some, such as CSA, are part of a much broader movement, which began in Japan in the 1970s, spread to Europe and then the US and Canada in the 1980s, where there are now 1,500 CSAs. Local farmers markets are also growing in popularity: they provide an excellent venue for small-scale producers to meet residents and visitors and celebrate the seasonal harvest. Discovery and revival of traditional and historic foods is engaging local communities and visitors in a growing network that supports sustainable food systems.

Networks for innovation

Collaboration is the key to food production and distribution; it is not possible to develop food systems without linking with community, non-profit, tourism, education and land management agencies. Community and youth groups that grow traditional foods in community gardens are bringing people into the local food network. Non-profit organisations such as the Native Movement, Native Seed Search and Slow Food USA are important partners in providing knowledge and advice on production of traditional foods. Schools, hospitals and universities also play a role in researching and educating the public about local food, while national and state park agencies have a vested interest in conserving the environment where wild food and animals exist. Finally, tour operators, festival organisers, restaurants and food enthusiasts engage and support local producers and wild food foragers.

Hence, sustainable food networks are extensive and interact with a wide cross-section of people in government, the community and business. Indeed, growing these networks could be considered just as important as growing the food that provides the focus of their efforts and the 'local flavour' of Arizona.

The links between place and produce will need to be protected from over-exploitation, especially when premium prices are obtained from the niche markets that consume these heritage foods. In order to do so, the CSE recommend adopting a system of geographic indications (GIs) that certify a product is from a certain place and maintains a level of quality, in the same way that European Union countries market their food and beverages. This will require an extensive marketing network supported by state and federal bodies that endorse trademarks, brands and labels. Other collaborations involve integration into interpretation and education programs at parks and museums, developing more county, tribal and local festivals that promote heritage foods and cultural traditions, dedicated university extension programs to assist in the development of value-added heritage foods, forming farmer-owned co-operatives for alternative and heritage crop production, incorporating heritage food themes into school curricula and developing broader collaborations across the food value chain (Nabhan, West & Pirog 2005).

Summary

The long-term vision of CSE is to ensure that heritage foods remain authentic, economically viable, sustainable, and thereby available to future generations (Nabhan, West & Pirog 2005). This will only be achieved when the numerous benefits of local food production are clearly identified, promoted, protected and supported. The process of strengthening local food systems involves many innovative initiatives and a wide range of stakeholders from the Native American, Hispanic, farming and urban communities. Reviving local food production involves many barriers, not the least of which is reversing consumer trends towards mass produced food and protecting farming and natural areas from invasion. Protection of the integrity and sustainability of the product is also vital, and a system similar to the GI used in Europe has been proposed. Finally, extensive and inclusive networks are critical to the revival and survival of heritage food production and the associated cultural traditions.

References

Carlsen, J & Edwards, D 2008, 'BEST EN case studies: Innovation for sustainable tourism', *Tourism and Hospitality Research* 8(1): 44-55.

Nabhan, GP, West, P & Pirog, R 2005, *Linking Arizona's Sense of Place to a Sense of Taste: Marketing the Heritage Value of Arizona's Place-Based Foods*, Centre for Sustainable Environments, Northern Arizona University.

Northern Arizona University website, accessed 31 March 2008, http://home.nau.edu/ environment/default.asp.

Chapter 7

EDDA

Facilitating innovation among Danish attractions

Anja Hergesell, Janne J Liburd and Jane Hansen

INTRODUCTION

In Denmark, the built attraction market is characterised by increasing professionalism and co-operation among suppliers who are also competitors in the global tourism and experience industry (Danish Ministry of Economic and Business Affairs 2004). Attempting to capitalise on the current trend toward a user-oriented, experience-driven economy that embraces 'soft' aspects like identity, feelings, values, meanings, and aesthetics for which customers are willing to pay more, a four-year project (2004-2008) entitled 'Experience Development of Danish Attractions' (EDDA) was initiated. EDDA (or ODA in Danish) connected thirty-eight built attractions of varying size, theme and ownership structure that joined forces to meet upcoming challenges and opportunities through shared competence development and incremental innovation. During the four-year project, product innovation took place in the form of altered or new tourism commodities and services. In addition, the attractions demonstrated their readiness to innovate by involving all personnel in the development of competences. Innovativeness was thus extended from mere product development to new aspects of management structures.

This case study reports on the EDDA project relations and structured patterns of interaction for innovative learning and competence development. Underpinning the dynamic sociocultural and economic aspects of sustainable tourism, the analysis focuses on how the much neglected principles of inter-generational and intra-generational equity also contributed to 'socially inclusive wealth creation'

(European University Association 2007, p. 21) by networking with a wide range of stakeholders.

Drivers of innovation

Recognising the economic opportunities associated with customers demanding unique, memorable and individualised experiences in the 'experience economy' (Pine II and Gilmore 1999), the Danish Government (2003) encouraged the development of new products and services as part of a national growth strategy. Generally requiring a limited upfront investment, if any at all, the experience economy has become of pivotal importance in driving the agenda for built attractions and tourism in Denmark at large. Moreover, the limited growth potential of the Danish attraction market (Danish Ministry of Economic and Business Affairs 2004) and an increasing number of highly professional experience providers direct the need for competence development and innovation, as:

- competition becomes increasingly fierce, both among built attractions and with other types of experience providers, including game manufacturers and retailers; and

- customer expectations are increasingly complex and multifaceted, which makes it difficult to satisfy consumers.

Although performing at a satisfactory level, the built attractions in Denmark recognised the need for acting proactively. The EDDA initiative aimed to support the attractions' sustainable development as strong and innovative businesses by creating opportunities for competence development and experience exchange. Acknowledging learning as a necessity for skills development and prerequisite for innovation, attractions worked together as colleagues while simultaneously respecting each other's originality, unique needs and opportunities.

A 'down to earth' development approach was adopted, i.e. project activities had to be inspirational and possible to implement by the EDDA participants. Moreover, embedded in a formulated framework of strategies, products and business plans, the critical importance of employees to facilitate memorable experiences was acknowledged as a key factor. This was reflected in the priority given to developing the skills of all personnel. However, memorable experience provision in the tourism industry is not only linked to individuals, but also results from interaction among individuals. Capitalising on both of these, the EDDA project was designed to explore innovation through the creativity of individuals and groups, the latter in the form of both internal and external partnerships. The project hence also contributed to 'socially inclusive wealth creation' (European University Association 2007, p. 21) by extending the project to the widest possible range of stakeholders.

Barriers to innovation

The EDDA project encountered a number of challenges, some of which are directly attributable to a lack of financial and human resources in the participating attractions. Limited human resources impeded the participation of staff in courses, study trips, experiential discussion groups and mentor-mentee relationships, which overall inhibited learning by individuals and hence uptake of innovation by the businesses. Due to the great variations in course attendance, a limitation on the number of participants per attraction was introduced to ensure equitable relationships, which is also a key principle in sustainable tourism development (Liburd 2007). In some instances, lack of funding constrained the implementation of newly acquired knowledge and tools, especially in the smaller attractions, which further had a negative impact on staff motivation.

Other barriers were overcome by the effective use of communication, including:

- reluctance and skepticism by several employees and managers about the usefulness of the project and the proposed changes, which led to one attraction leaving EDDA after a change of management;
- lack of understanding regarding the adopted approach, which was occasionally considered irrelevant to the built attractions' context;
- lack of active contribution and commitment, which resulted in the exclusion of a second participant; and
- inability of some external lecturers to adapt their course content to reflect the needs of the built attractions.

Finally, the geographic dimension of the project involving participants from all over Denmark (see Map 7.1) constituted an organisational obstacle. This was handled by arranging activities in various regions of the country and making effective use of online communication, especially the project website www.odaweb.dk.

Processes for innovation

Originally, the EDDA project was envisioned by four attraction managers who had previously worked together on competence development. They sought financial support from the Danish Labor Market Holiday Fund and received a sizeable sum of 36 million Danish Kroner (approximately 5 million Euros). Participating attractions co-financed an additional 10 million Danish Kroner (approx. 1.1 million Euros). Forty built attractions were selected based on location, size, theme and ownership structure. Two all-day seminars marked the starting point of EDDA, where each participating attraction presented its expectations for project contents and outcomes. Based on the findings, a learning program was created which incorporated four key elements:

- *Knowledge and tools:* generation of knowledge (e.g. through surveys) and development of tools (e.g. books) to support the implementation of innovations in products, services and management processes;
- *Professional courses:* development and implementation of tailor-made modules including case studies and study trips, designed on basis of initial interview findings and anticipated knowledge gaps;

- *Networking activities including thematic discussion groups and mentor-mentee relationship building:* opportunities for employees and managers to exchange experiences and enhance group learning; and

- *Support for implementation:* funding allocated for professional individual consultancy.

Map 7.1 Location of the 38 participating attractions

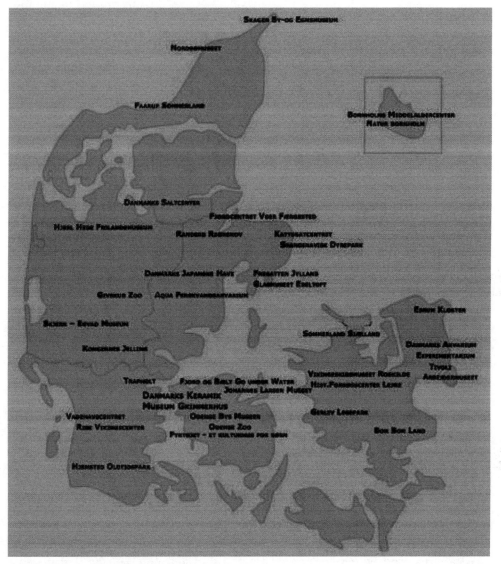

Source: Adapted from EDDA Secretariat.

Over four and a half years the EDDA project was carried out in three main stages:

1. Phase I (January 2004-July 2005) on the development of key competences for the design of strategies to create competitive attractions;

2. Phase II (August 2005-July 2006) on the development of experiences; and

3. Phase III (August 2006-July 2008) on project consolidation and the implementation of innovations in participating attractions.

To secure a satisfactory project outcome, participant evaluations were conducted at the end of each course and of each phase. If possible, adjustments were made to meet expectations and business needs. Moreover, EDDA was regularly monitored by external auditors. The Danish Institute of Technology periodically evaluated project outcomes and ongoing learning processes, including participants' satisfaction rate, which exceeded an impressive 90 percent.

Based on the three-tiered project structure, numerous activities were scheduled, including courses and workshops, study trips, analyses and book publications, networking opportunities and conferences. Most of these activities took place throughout the duration of the project, but varied in frequency. More than 2,000 participants attended the 65 courses and workshops which covered topics like leadership and HR, service management and business development, experience development, and communication and marketing. Site visits were conducted over several days to attractions in Denmark, Germany, the United Kingdom, Spain, the Netherlands, Norway and France. Useful outputs also include a series of handbooks on management aspects (event management, PR, market research, sponsorship, volunteers, customer survey manuals, etc.) and several books on selected aspects of attraction development such as strategy design, storytelling and experience development. Moreover, tools to estimate the contribution of attractions to the region's economy and employment were developed to strengthen the position of attractions as regionally important actors. All books, analyses and materials related to the courses and study trips were made accessible on the project website for participants and non-participating tourism providers in Denmark. They have continued to be freely available to anyone after project termination. EDDA thus continues to be of inspiration to attractions and other tourism businesses in Denmark.

EDDA has not only addressed other tourism professionals in Denmark through the openly available website information but has also successfully engaged project externals in a number of meetings on experience development and in the semiannual conferences. This also served to broaden the scope of knowledge generation and dissemination. Nevertheless, the major focus of the project has been the inclusion of all personnel from participating attractions in the competence development process. Individual employees were encouraged to attend courses and to get involved outside of the classroom, for instance by joining one of the experiential discussion groups. Phase III of the project specifically focused on networking as a method of learning. During that phase a mentor-mentee program was established and thematic networks on, for example, change management and trends in the attraction sector were established with participants from inside and outside of the EDDA network. In addition, by 'training the trainers' the project strived to ensure that knowledge was distributed to all personnel and that innovations were implemented. This approach proved particularly effective in a combination of professional advice from tourism consultants, who were self-selected by the participating attractions.

Networks for innovation

Networks lay at the core of EDDA, as the underlying principle of the project was to encourage innovativeness through intra- and inter-organisational learning. The 38 participating attractions varied in geographical location, size, ownership structure and thematic focus (the latter ranged from cultural heritage and art as well as flora and fauna, to amusement and edutainment, i.e. experiences that combine education with elements of entertainment). Project activities, such as courses (including training of the trainers), conferences, study trips, experiential discussion groups and the mentor-mentee program resulted in intra- and inter-organisational relationship building. During these activities and through the formation of networks the principles of inter- and intra-generational equity were enacted. While being competitors, the benefits of sharing and disseminating knowledge were clearly recognised by participants. This may also be attributed to the emphasis placed on respecting the needs for communication and business opportunities of individual participants while engaging in joint experiences of learning in multiple environments.

Benkler (2006, p. 369), in 'The Wealth of Networks', stated that 'communication is constitutive of social relations'. There can be no relationships, and thereby no networks, without communicating with others. Some modes of communication and networking were based on face-to-face interaction; others, though, were online exchanges including texts and images that were easily transmitted at distance, frequently without the presence of voice, and almost never involving touch, smell or taste. Other differences in communication modes and forms of networking beyond the technical were culturally or organisationally embedded, which imply that certain values, structures of control, power and knowledge inform how and with whom we communicate and establish networks. The dialectic relationship between the individual attractions and the power of a formal project structure greatly contributed to the creation of employee networks that were creative and innovative. Innovations exploit changes (Hjalager 2010, p. 149). In other words, based on the dynamic principles of sociocultural and economic sustainability, creativity, learning and innovation were supported by network formation and embedded in the project design.

Initially established by four Danish built attractions to encourage innovation in the sector, the leading organisation behind the EDDA project was the Development Fund for Tourist Attractions, financially supported by the Labor Market Holiday Fund in Denmark. While the organisation's board was responsible for the overall project implementation, the daily management was assigned to the Experience Development Centre under the auspices of a regional DMO. Consisting of representatives from various public and private tourism development and marketing entities, the Experience Development Centre functioned as a secretariat-type network, which was headed by one of this chapter's co-authors, Jane Hansen. Additional external networks for innovation were established through the implementation of project activities. Both academics and practitioners were involved in the design and delivery of courses. Outside of the classroom, participating attractions selected individual consultants to help bridge the gap between theory and practice where necessary. All consultants were listed in a shared database. Moreover, study trips to non-participating tourism attractions in Denmark and abroad as well as conference presentations by delegates from outside the EDDA network have initiated national and international relationship building that could further inspire inter-organisational learning. In supporting these processes, the project website, newsletters, conferences and books have been of key importance.

Summary

EDDA was driven by a mission to develop competences in a comprehensive and innovative manner among all personnel at the built attractions, whose core offer is delivering good experiences, in order to meet future demand and thereby to sustain their businesses. Next to the actively involved participants, the EDDA project established links to other national and international tourism stakeholders. Knowledge and tools on sustaining competitive businesses and specifically on creating good experiences were developed and disseminated through courses, study trips, networks and the use of electronic and print media. Knowledge transfer and creativity by individuals and in groups were key to successful innovation in products, services and management processes in the built attractions, thus following the principles of socially inclusive wealth creation by taking due account of the complexities of learning and society at large. Rather than being grounded in the past or the complacency of the present, EDDA's mission and activities were future-orientated. Since the Danish attractions were not overtly affected by the outcomes of unsustainable practices and lack of innovation they still chose to act, as opposed to being pressed into action when it is too late to do anything. This also implies that the sustainable development of tourism is a dynamic process of change, rather than a static goal to be achieved (Liburd & Edwards 2010).

Establishing creative networks to help drive innovation for sustainable tourism, EDDA envisioned a follow-up project that could effectively enhance competence development and innovation among other tourism providers in Denmark. A three-year project, from 2010 to 2013, entitled the Experience Academy (see the website www.oplevelsernesacademy.dk) was initiated by the regional DMO of Southern Denmark (Syddansk Turisme). Financially supported by the EU and the project partners (24 teaching institutions, 22 municipalities and more than 160 tourism businesses), the project provides a comprehensive overview of existing offers of further training relevant to the tourism industry. Moreover, it organised and delivered a range of courses on all levels, particularly in the area of experience development. Seminars, conferences, sector-specific meetings and a range of networking activities continue to encourage intra- and inter-organisational learning as a prerequisite for innovation. Hence, various elements of the EDDA project were adopted in this follow-up project. Moreover, some of the former participants of the EDDA project were involved in the follow-up project as partners and advisory board members.

In summary, while the EDDA project was initially limited to a group of 38 individual tourist attractions, the lessons learned were not restricted to this group. Adhering to the principles of inter- and intra-generational equity they continue to be of inspiration to tourism enterprises in Denmark, as well as to tourism businesses abroad, that are looking to enhance their innovative competences in a context of growing global competition, changing consumer demands and calls for more sustainable practices.

References

Benkler, Y 2006, *The Wealth of Networks*, Yale University Press, New Haven.

Danish Government 2003, *Denmark in the Culture and Experience Economy – 5 new steps* Danish Ministry of Economic and Business Affairs, Copenhagen, 6 February 2008, www.oem.dk/publication/dk-culture/experience_economy.pdf.

Danish Ministry of Economic and Business Affairs 2004, *Analyse af det danske turismeerhverv*, Ramboll, Virum, accessed 31 January 2008, www.upload.pls.ramboll.dk/dan/Publikationer/Oplevelsesokonomi/Turismera pporten.pdf.

EDDA Secretariat n.d., *EDDA*, Experience Development Centre, Odense, accessed 31 August 2011, www.odaweb.dk.

European University Association 2007, *Creativity in higher education: Report on the EUA creativity project 2006-2007*, European University Association, Brussels, accessed 8 January 2008, www.eua.be.

Hjalager, A-M 2010, 'Supplier-driven Innovations for Sustainable Tourism', in JJ Liburd & D Edwards (eds), *Understanding the Sustainable Development of Tourism*, Goodfellow Publishers, Oxford: 148-162.

Liburd, JJ 2007, 'Sustainable tourism, cultural practice and competence development for hotels and inns in Denmark', *Tourism Recreation Research* 32(1): 41-48.

Liburd, JJ & Edwards, D (eds) 2010, *Understanding the Sustainable Development of Tourism*, Goodfellow Publishers, Oxford.

Syddansk Turisme n.d., *Oplevelsernes Academy*, Syddansk Turisme, Middlefart, accessed 22 August 2011, www.oplevelsernesacademy.dk.

Pine II, BJ & Gilmore, JH 1999, *The experience economy: Work is theatre and every business a stage*, Harvard Business School Press, Boston.

Chapter 8

Brenu Beach Resort
Innovation for financial independence

MICHAEL KWEKU COMMEH AND NICO SCHULENKORF

INTRODUCTION

In August 2001, the New Patriotic Party (NPP) had assumed power in Ghana. One of the reasons for the NPP's success was the promise to invest in and develop the local economy under the slogan 'Golden Age of Business', especially among the private sector community. The change towards a new democratic government resulted in wide-ranging goodwill from the local population, who were expecting a new level of personal and professional freedom in Ghana. The business sector was longing for positive change, as for almost 30 years private businesses had not received significant support from the preceding governments. People in the tourism industry were finally encouraged to invest into their innovative business ideas and motivated to start up small enterprises to increase their quality of life.

Originality, creativity and appropriateness are generally described as key elements for innovation. While innovation is associated with the introduction of new ideas or concepts, geographers use the expression 'coping strategies' when describing innovation under difficult social circumstances (Yaro 2004). In Ghana, for most entrepreneurs in the tourism sector the term innovation is part of daily life's 'coping', or a constant survival process. People practice innovation to survive in their business environment, and they alter and adapt according to the resources available – a process which, in Ghanaian, is represented by the Akan Adinkra twisting symbol *Nkyinkyim* meaning dynamism and versatility. Ghanaians believe that these characteristics underlie the resourcefulness of mankind, and that one changes and adapts as life evolves (Bodomo *et al.* 2010). The definition of innovation adopted by Auntie Aggie, the entrepreneur featured in this case study, is 'creating something meaningful out of nothing for a specific purpose or aim, using available and appropriate resources' (first author, personal communication).

The small ecotourism business 'Brenu Beach Resort', established by Auntie Aggie and located on an attractive beach area at the Komenda Eguafo Edina Abirim District, is investigated in this case study. Auntie Aggie's ecotourism business is an innovative contribution to tourism in Ghana. As a lack of resources limited her business capabilities and led her to establish an open air do-it-yourself chop bar and restaurant, where tourists could have something to eat when they came to spend time at the beach. A chop bar can be described as a traditional local restaurant where food is prepared and served in less than a minute. Typical Ghanaian dishes are cooked in such restaurants and are generally eaten with the hands. The tourists were encouraged to contribute to the meals and do their own cooking by using the basic cooking utensils provided and enjoy the authentic style of dining. For accommodation, visitors were encouraged to set up a camp site on the beach area or build huts from coconut branches. Over twenty years Brenu Beach Resort has evolved from a single hut restaurant, to a self-styled open air beach restaurant and guest house.

Drivers of innovation

From the seven informal interviews conducted with Auntie Aggie, three outstanding features were eminent which drive innovation in her case: the survival instinct of human beings; the balance between demand and supply; and the trustful interrelationships among all the stakeholders in the tourism industry. First, considering the need to look after her three children and provide a place for them to stay, Auntie Aggie followed her survival instinct. It was her strong will to first finance her children's education and be financially independent, which encouraged her to creatively use the few natural resources available to her. With a supportive family and a local beach area to utilise, ecotourism appeared to be a promising opportunity for professional success. Auntie Aggie had observed a rising demand for authentic Ghanaian tourism when an increasing number of local and foreign visitors complained about inadequate food and accommodation in the area. International tourists, in particular, were longing for authentic, traditional and yet convenient overnight shelters, which would add to their cultural experiences.

Second, the balance between supply and demand was a crucial driver for innovation. The tourists represent the demand side, while the supply side consists of service providers that offer accommodation, food, artefacts, tour guides and other tourism functions. To maximise performance, the tourists should be at least satisfied with their experience, while the entrepreneurs realise a satisfactory return on investment through the products and services they provide (Commeh 1999). For example, if the tourist seeks to enjoy an unspoiled clean beach or have firsthand experience of authentic cooking, and if the provider can deliver to his standards, then satisfaction is likely. In this case, if tourists were happy with the services Auntie Aggie provided and if they valued her performance, then they would leave satisfied and may come again and/or encourage others to visit the beach resort.

Third, a key factor for innovative co-operation was the trustful relationships between players in the tourism arena, which result from good business contacts and supportive local networks. Informing stakeholders of their importance to sustainable tourism development and rewarding achievers and performers are crucial actions that may eventually result in further innovative practices. At the same time, co-operation with important stakeholders in the community will guarantee support among the local people, other tourism providers and the local government. In Ghana, local community networks and co-operation between key players in the industry are still developing, which at times made life difficult for Auntie Aggie.

Barriers to innovation

From a micro-economic perspective, a family or traditionally owned beach area provided Auntie Aggie with the basic physical resources needed to start her ecotourism business. However, there were no financial means to establish appropriate guesthouse facilities. While a beautiful coastline, a two-and-a-half-kilometre-long beach, marine life and a large tract of undeveloped land were available, the essential means and structures needed to develop a small resort were missing. Apart from the beach, Auntie Aggie's only resources when opening the chop bar and restaurant were cooking utensils such as charcoal pots and three traditional cooking stones. The lack of financial and material assets proved to be an initial barrier to innovation. It was this lack of resources that encouraged her to be creative and to identify alternative opportunities, such as the 'do-it-yourself' chop bar.

From a macro-economic perspective, a lack of support and the staggering interventions of the previous Ghanaian governments presented some of the greatest barriers to innovations in Ghanaian tourism. In the 1980s and early 1990s, the tourism sector grew at a rate of 3.5 to 5 percent, and then began to accelerate in the late 1990s. Under the proactive and business-orientated government, the macro-economic performance improved significantly. Recording an immense revenue of US$1.6 billion by 2010, tourist expenditure is said to have been growing year-on-year since 2002 (the year the Tourism Council began tracking statistics), and receipts reached over US$b a year, translating into about 6.7 percent of the nation's Gross Domestic Product (GDP), with an annual growth rate of about 6.6 percent (Investment in Ghana 2010). This can be related to the positive changes in politics, a stable political system, and policies that have improved the overall wellbeing of the tourism industry (Gartner 1999, 2000, 2001 and 2005).

Generally, sociocultural barriers to innovation can occur if host communities, government and local authorities do not adequately support tourism (Kiss 2004). For instance, in some cases the chief of a community can decide to intervene destructively, as was the case with Auntie Aggie's business. When her business became popular with both local and foreign tourists, the Central Regional Development Commission intruded by building a tourist centre and a guesthouse right next to her chop bar. So, instead of receiving support for her own business, the entrepreneur found herself struggling with newly introduced competitive, social and financial barriers. The community chief did not approve the expansion of her business to a larger guest house or motel. Auntie Aggie believed that the main reasons for these restrictions were (a) her unwillingness to pay money (and bribes) for land titles to the chiefs and (b) leaders' personal frustration in seeing a woman establish a successful business. The restrictions experienced caused a drastic reduction in her potential income, which again set new barriers to further innovation and sustainable socioeconomic development.

Processes of innovation

There are four main processes which contribute to a continuously innovative social and economic tourism business environment. These are:

- the provision of adequate education that encourages creative thinking;
- the use of up-to-date technology;
- the rule of law; and
- financial incentives.

First, education is considered the foundation of a sustainable society, and it will be the most influential determinant of the success or failure of tourism businesses (Greenspan 2007). Allan Greenspan, former chair of the US Federal Reserve Bank, when advising middle school students, said: 'The solution to some of our gravest problems lies in reforming the way we educate our children' (Greenspan 2007: 344-345). He (2007) further explained that education can also help businesses to 'creatively destroy' and revitalise themselves from within by scrapping old and failing projects and then reallocating resources to newer, more productive ones. By helping people understand the dynamics of the field in which they operate, resources can be more efficiently and creatively allocated to meet the new market dynamics.

Second, technology in today's world is changing so fast that the direction of change is unpredictable. As a developing country, Ghana is not an exception, and it was crucial for the country to be proactive with new and innovative infrastructural development projects. Communication technology – for example mobile phones, the internet, cable TV – has arguably turned the global village into a small ghetto. In rural Ghana, the development of information technology and infrastructure had recently allowed larger enterprises to increase direct communication and virtual presence via internet sites, emails and mobile phones. However, for small tourism businesses without information technology access, opportunities for attracting and targeting customers remain low, which resulted in an increasing competitive disadvantage. Government support for investments into technology was therefore seen as a crucial driver for socioeconomic prosperity.

Third, applying the rule of law and order would ensure the safety and trustworthiness of a sustainable business environment. For example, once prevailing issues and uncertainty regarding land ownership and property rights in Ghana are resolved, the tourism industry can operate freely and under just circumstances. Such macro-factors are crucial for attracting and securing tourist providers and business people who are interested in investing in the local economy. A functioning, reliable and non-corrupt government will secure law and order for the benefit of the local people and contractors. If all misbehaviour is dealt with, fairly and justly, trust within business sectors and communities can be created and opportunities for investments will grow.

Fourth, financial incentives and support by local and national governments were considered vital measures for advancing innovation, particularly in a developing country such as Ghana. Often, the local entrepreneurs did not possess the initial resources necessary to establish a business or company, and individuals with creative and innovative ideas are often limited in their power to realise and implement their business plans due to associated expenses. Here, the government was encouraged to provide a support frame for small businesses by facilitating investments, which should encourage and benefit newly established local entrepreneurs and their workforce. Initial subsidies, incentives and support would encourage small entrepreneurship.

Networks for innovation

The creation of integrative tourism networks was fundamental for the effective exchange and advancement of information, ideas and projects among players in the tourism industry. Networks could be both the source and beneficiary of the different processes needed to establish an innovative socioeconomic environment in Ghana. Existing contacts and networks can open doors and propel the growth of the tourism industry, whilst the togetherness of people, the exchange of ideas and the co-operation in projects can lead to new friendships and networks being created for future tasks (Bortei-Doku Aryeetey 1998).

Networking in Ghana was not appropriately understood as (a) a form of effective exchange of information for the advancement of developmental goals and (b) a process and tool for effective good practices that engender good governance. For example, rather than receiving help and advice from other players in the tourism industry, the benefits Auntie Aggie obtained from networking comes from the good rapport and regular exchange she has with her customers. The tourists often gave her ideas and support on how to run her business effectively and what and how to change or innovate. For instance, tourists have mentioned the importance of having an internet site and an email to enable her to market and promote her business on a larger scale. Tourists were also posting their positive experience at Auntie Aggie's Beach Resort on internet travel platforms and blogging sites.

On the issue of good practices and good governance, networking is capable of bringing together common ethical values that will foster trust, effective communication and understanding among local, national and international stakeholders (O'Riordan & Stoll-Kleemann 2002; Stoker 1998). Considering the ambiguity of language as Derrida's (1967) deconstruction posits, dialogue among stakeholders in the network can be efficient and effective through self-reflection, in which pragmatic communication (Agyekum 2012), forms a crucial role. The individual actors and groups within the network have acquired certain experiences and understanding that are formed from their social environment. These unique experiences are normally in a particular context. It is through networking between an array of different actors and groups with multiple perspectives that problems can be assessed effectively and efficiently on common ethical ground (Pretty & Pimbert 1995).

On a macro scale, it remains to be seen how the government, financial institutions, tourism researchers and entrepreneurs share innovative ideas amongst each other. If these tourism stakeholders see the value of co-operating, supporting and linking to each other in innovative ways, then socioeconomic development is likely (Bortei-Doku Aryeetey 1998). People can learn from each other, avoid common problems or co-operate to overcome barriers, trouble or hardships. At the same time, networking can help to improve or strengthen rules and regulations that support effective innovations. This could, for example, encourage financial institutions to support the industry, once a certain macro-framework is provided and a strong intra-industrial network is established.

If networks in the Ghanaian tourism industry had been well coordinated and properly functioning, Auntie Aggie would not have experienced the same level of mishaps and problems along the way. For example, land title registration problems and miscommunication between her and the local chiefs could have been avoided if an intra-community network had been available to support her. Local businesses could have exchanged experiences and assisted each other during the registration processes and in dealing with government officials. Employing an effective and culturally acceptable local network promises to be a convincing strategy towards solving complex community issues and overcoming sociocultural differences.

Summary

This case study discussed the underlying relations of power and socioeconomic systems influencing innovation in tourism in the context of Ghana's evolving young democracy. The study featured a female entrepreneur, whose innovative ecotourism business managed to overcome financial, social and cultural barriers. Co-operation and networking between individuals, communities, tourism operators and government officials promises to be beneficial for small-scale tourism developments in the country. While the relationships between stakeholders in the industry are currently loose or non-existent, the establishment of local networks can help to effectively promote information flow, share knowledge, and establish contact and trust between all tourism stakeholders. The Government is encouraged to contribute to innovative developments by establishing a macro-frame for the community including the provision of education, technology and financial incentives. The effective exchange of information among all stakeholders in the tourism industry would allow contacts and networks to be established and trends to be anticipated and addressed.

In summary, factors that promote or hinder innovation can be complex, especially in a developing world context, where traditional and cultural systems considerably influence socioeconomic development and transformation processes toward more sustainable practice. Innovative ideas and policies can have a positive impact on the social, cultural, economic and political environment. However, it remains to be seen if the local micro-business environment and local entrepreneurs, like Aunt Aggie, can continue to benefit if projects are not sufficiently supported by governments.

References

Agyekum, K 2012, 'Polite Language': Towards Perfect Communication, National Cohesion and Peaceful Co-Existence, 23 February, www.ug.edu.gh/index1.php?linkid=213&archiveid=1015&page=1&adate=Thu.%3Cbr%20%2F%3EFeb.%2023.

Bodomo, A, Marfo, C & Hall-Lew, L 2010, *Let's speak Twi: A proficiency course in Akan language and culture*, CSLI, Stanford.

Bortei-Doku Aryeetey, E 1998, 'Consultative processes in community development in Northern Ghana', *Community Development Journal* 33(4): 301-313.

Commeh, MK 1999, *The enhancement of eco-tourism small scale businesses in a sustainable way, using Geographic Information System, in Kwazulu-Natal province, South Africa*, MSc thesis, Universität Flensburg, Germany.

Derrida, J (1967) 1974, *Of Grammatology*, Gayatri Spivak (trans.), The Johns Hopkins University Press, Baltimore.

Gartner WC 1999, 2000, 2001 & 2005, 'Small Scale Enterprises in Tourism Industry in Ghana's Central Region', in DG Pearce and RW Burtler (eds), *Contemporary Issues in Tourism Development*, Routledge, New York.

Greenspan, A 2007, *The Age of Turbulence – Adventures in a New World*, Penguin Press, New York: 344-345.

Investing in Ghana 2010, *The UK-Ghana Investment Forum 2010*, www.developingmarkets.com/dma/wpcontent/uploads/2010/07/investing-in-ghana-2010.pdf.

O'Riordan, T & Stoll-Kleemann, S 2002, *Biodiversity, Sustainability and Human Communities - Protecting beyond the Protected*, Cambridge University Press: 93-106.

Pretty, MP & Pimbert, JN 1995, *Parks, People and Professionals: Putting Participation into Protected Areas Management*, United Nations Research Institute for Social Development, Geneva.

Stoker, G 1998, 'Governance as theory', *International Social Science Journal* 155: 17-28.

Chapter 9

Asian German Sports Exchange Programme
Innovative social sporting networks

NICO SCHULENKORF

INTRODUCTION

The Asian German Sports Exchange Programme (AGSEP) is an NGO which has been conducting sport events and international exchanges between Sri Lankan and European sport teams since 1989. The organisation is based in Marawila, in rural western Sri Lanka, and was founded by its current CEO, Dr Dietmar Döring, who at that time was the national coach of the Sri Lankan table tennis team. Dr Döring saw an opportunity to use sport events as an avenue to enhance tourism in the area, whilst fostering the relationships between international and local sportspeople, and among the estranged ethnic communities in Sri Lanka.

The philosophy of AGSEP is that sport provides an exciting tool for connecting people and transcending social, cultural, ethnic and religious divides. Sport provides a vehicle for all participants to share experiences and learn from each other in a playful and open atmosphere. AGSEP stages international large-scale events (such as football tournaments or intercultural festivals) three to four times a year, while small-scale event projects and inter-ethnic exchanges for schoolchildren from the different areas of post-war Sri Lanka take place on a fortnightly basis.

AGSEP is headquartered in the premises of the Aquarius Resort, a sport hotel complex which was built by Dr Döring and his partners in 1989 and is now managed and operated by local Sri Lankan staff. Over the years, the resort grew from 12 rooms and 12 local staff members to 40 rooms and over 40 staff. The Aquarius Resort's close co-operation with AGSEP guarantees a steady influx of tourists including sport teams and their entourages, who participate in sport exchanges and reside at the resort during their stay in Sri Lanka.

Against the background of a long-lasting civil war and inter-ethnic tensions in the country, community sport event tourism provides an innovative and sustainable form of development in rural Sri Lanka. This type of active tourism has a socio-cultural focus and combines people's travel experiences with the emotional factor of contributing to the advancement of intercultural understanding and peace in a divided country. Whereas sport events themselves are not entirely new to tourism, AGSEP innovatively uses friendly matches between international sport teams and the Sri Lankan teams to advance sport skills and local capacities and contribute to overall community development. Some of the socioeconomic benefits resulting from the sport event tourism program include the promotion of the destination and an increase in jobs and revenue for the local community. In other words, AGSEP attracts international tourists and sport clubs on a regular basis to the touristically unattractive and often neglected rural town of Marawila, which benefits the local community and in particular the small business owners and tourist operators.

Drivers of innovation

For more than 25 years, civil war and political struggle between the Sinhalese-dominated Sri Lankan Government and the Liberation Tigers of Tamil Eelam (known as LTTE or Tamil Tigers) severely hindered any form of sustainable social, cultural and economic development in the country. Often described as the most violent and dirty ethnic conflict in modern states, Sri Lanka's civil war resulted in over 100,000 casualties. Even after the defeat of the Tamil Tigers and the official end of the civil war in 2009, intergroup relations among Sri Lanka's ethnic groups remain deeply shattered and the desire for active, peaceful and fun-bringing activities remains a priority for everyone involved in promoting reconciliation and socioeconomic development in post-war Sri Lanka.

Dr Döring's idea of combining tourism with integrative sport events may well provide such an active platform. This claim is supported by a growing body of theoretical and empirical research that shows sport's potential as a mechanism for conflict resolution and peace-building (Gasser & Levinsen 2004; Kidd 2008; Schulenkorf 2010b; Sugden 2006). Driven by the desire to 'make a difference' in Sri Lanka, AGSEP defines integrative sport events as peaceful intergroup sport encounters that popularise social values such as intercultural togetherness, respect, courage, commitment, and appreciation through active participation and exchange. All of their integrative sport events are planned, organised and implemented in co-operation with stakeholders from the three major ethnic groups on the island: the Sinhalese, the Tamils and the Muslims. In addition to local communities, the event organisers target international sport tourists who want to actively contribute to the reconciliation process in Sri Lanka by participating in peace-building sport and event encounters.

Three main types of benefits arise from the integrative community sport event tourism projects. Firstly, the interaction of different people working towards the common goal of staging a successful sport event is expected to create collective feelings of togetherness, passion, identity and community, which are particularly important for the processes of reconciliation and peace-building (see Schulenkorf 2010b; Sugden 2006). In other words, intercultural participation may enhance intergroup understanding, appreciation and reciprocal learning, and therefore lead to ongoing social and cultural development. Secondly, from a psychological perspective, participating local groups may experience a sense of accomplishment and pride when successfully staging inter-community events. Against the background of a severely disadvantaged community setting, the mere organisation of sport events in rural Sri Lanka presents a great achievement and is certainly an experience out of the norm for everyone involved. Thirdly, larger sport events attract international participants and tourists who add to the international flair of the events and may contribute to the socioeconomic development of the local community. In this case, sport event tourists generate financial benefits for the Aquarius Resort, tourism operators, local shops and other businesses in rural Marawila.

Barriers to innovation

There have been many external and internal barriers for AGSEP to overcome in the development and staging of international events and intergroup sport projects. First, the frequent change of the socio-political circumstances and the varying safety and security situation in Sri Lanka have presented significant external challenges. For many years, a latent risk of terrorist attacks has been prevalent at all events, particularly at large festivals and tournaments staged in the war-torn northeast of Sri Lanka. Up until 2009, AGSEP had to overcome this significant external barrier and had to decide strategically which communities to invite, and when and where to stage events. For example, during times of official civil war sport events with Tamil teams from north eastern Sri Lanka were only taking place in the western Sri Lankan community of Marawila – travel to LTTE-controlled areas was avoided. On the other hand, during times of official ceasefire, opportunities for negotiations between all parties (e.g. Government and LTTE sport councils) were taken and a number of integrative sport events were realised in the border town between Sinhalese- and Tamil-controlled land.

One of AGSEP's most significant wartime achievements was a women's soccer tournament in October 2003 which featured the Sri Lankan national team, a Tamil selection and the German club SV Herrmannstein. The event was held in the border town Vavuniya, which separated Government and LTTE controlled areas; it was the first event conducted in northern Sri Lanka for over 35 years and it attracted more than 10,000 local and international spectators (Gammanpila 2002). The few remaining hotels, hostels and guest houses in the area were fully booked for the first time in years, as tourist and visitor demand exceeded supply. However, it needs to be recognised that the preparation phase for the tournament lasted for almost two years, as permissions from several ministries (including the Ministry of Interior and Defence Ministry) were required, and support from a variety of stakeholders (including The Police, Red Cross, Tamil Sports Council, etc.) was needed to allow for a safe event environment. More recently, the fear of terrorism decreased following the end of the civil war in 2009 and the subsequent lifting of the country's state of emergency status in September 2011. However, security and risk management remain at the forefront of all of AGSEP's event planning activities.

The second external barrier to innovation is the lack of infrastructure in many regional parts of Sri Lanka, including the rural western town of Marawila where AGSEP and the Aquarius Resort are located. Streets are in bad condition, public transport is unreliable and sport grounds are primitive by international standards. This barrier is partly overcome by an agreement between AGSEP and the Aquarius Resort which guarantees the use of a small-scale multi-sport ground in the premises of the resort for some of the outdoor events. Furthermore, in terms of transportation, two community-owned minibuses provide an opportunity to get international participants and visitors to the events more comfortably.

Internally, the biggest challenge for AGSEP and Aquarius Resort is the differences in socio-cultural values between Asian and European tourists and sport participants, including local customs such as food and nightlife. For example, whereas German or English sport teams are used to European-style food and heavy alcohol consumption, the Sri Lankans favour rice and curry – some of the young sport participants do not handle large amounts of alcohol well. In addition, there are cultural differences in valuing competitiveness and the desire to win at AGSEP events. European teams expect strong competition and a good workout – even when playing international friendly matches. On the contrary, Sri Lankans often take part in friendly matches for social and cultural reasons, and to enjoy the atmosphere of a truly international day. For them, sport is the means, not the end. This can be a significant problem when the level and strength of play are different, and European teams feel they are not challenged enough or embarrass the Sri Lankans in soaring defeat. To deal with this, Sri Lankan teams are now inspected by AGSEP staff before exchange trips, and their level of performance is analysed so that they can be matched with suitable teams from Europe.

The second major internal challenge is that of language. While the German CEO is able to communicate in English, his Sinhala is very basic and he does not possess any Tamil language skills. Additionally, not all locals are capable of understanding and speaking English fluently, and some have no English skills at all. Further complicating the problem, Sinhala and Tamil are two completely separate languages and often members of the two ethnic groups do not understand each other. Finally, the ethnic mix of staff (Sinhalese, Tamil, Muslim and European) prevalent at the Aquarius Resort is not the norm in Sri Lankan tourist companies. Against the background of a long-lasting civil war, ethnic prejudices, stereotypes and rivalries need to be overcome. For example, it took months of continuous engagement and non-verbal interaction before basic language skills were learnt and first signs of trust between all parties could be witnessed. While an inter-cultural workgroup may be of great advantage in the long term, communication and trust issues had a negative effect on co-operation and overall effectiveness in the short term.

Processes of innovation

AGSEP's sport event tourism and social development activities can be divided into two main phases. The first phase lasted from 1989 until 2002, throughout which the international sport exchange program was started and consequently advanced. The second phase commenced after the signing of the Cease Fire Agreement (CFA) between the Sri Lankan Government and the LTTE in 2002. Since then, AGSEP has been focusing predominantly on intra-Sri Lankan sport events, as well as peace and reconciliation efforts.

During the first phase, an international exchange program between Sri Lankan sport teams (mainly football, basketball, volleyball and table tennis) from the government-controlled western and southern parts of Sri Lanka and European sport clubs was established. The two main foci of this program were to provide positive socio-cultural overseas experiences for all participants, and to advance the development of outstanding athletes and coaches. For both Sri Lankan and European participants, the sport exchanges offered new and exciting cultural experiences, unique social opportunities with foreign people, and the chance of representing their country in an international context. During their visits to Sri Lanka, the European teams stayed at the Aquarius Resort. They were invited to look beyond the scope of the sport experience and combined their beach and sport holidays with activities such as visiting historic sites and cultural highlights of the island. These activities were organised and conducted by players from the local community and allowed local tourism providers to make some extra business. In return, when performing at sport matches in Europe, the Sri Lankan teams were accommodated and entertained free-of-charge by host families.

The other focus of the exchange program was on sport development and on the individual training and education of talented sports people and coaches. Selected Sri Lankan participants were invited to train with and learn from European sport experts and former professional players. The very best were given the opportunity to train with professional teams and sign overseas contracts to further their individual careers. At the same time, Sri Lankan sport coaches, trainers and support staff were invited to attend workshops, seminars and conferences to learn from experienced European coaching experts. Theoretical knowledge was combined with practical experience under a 'train the trainers' approach (see Burnett 2006). This multiplier strategy was implemented to secure future support of local sportspeople and clubs in Sri Lanka.

The second phase of AGSEP's sport projects started in 2002, after the signing of the CFA between the Sri Lankan Government and the LTTE rebels. Since then, AGSEP has been placing its focus on integrating sportspeople of Sri Lanka's rival ethnic groups in inter-community sport camps, sport events and workshops, to provide them with an opportunity to get to know and appreciate each other. In the first years, these sport-for-development activities were conducted exclusively on the Aquarius Resort premises in Marawila. More recently, peace and reconciliation projects have been realised in different parts of the island, including tournaments in the previously war-affected north-eastern parts of Sri Lanka where people are longing for sport activities and infrastructure. As a response, AGSEP, in co-operation with local communities and workers from the area, has constructed a multi-sport complex in Nilaveli, and first sport projects have started to emerge. While the centre is currently co-managed by AGSEP, it is anticipated that the local communities and tourism operators will be managing and sustaining the centre in the long term. It will be their task to learn from the 'event experts' with the final goal of being able to independently plan and organise exchanges, events and adjunct programs for tourists and visitors.

To realise a sustainable form of development, local communities need to be empowered by receiving an increased amount of responsibility over time. Furthermore, AGSEP needs to be committed to transferring power and control to the locals once they have prepared and trained for the upcoming challenges of event management and program ownership. The community empowerment approach underpinning this gradual development process is illustrated, with the Model of Community Empowerment, in Figure 9.1 (see Schulenkorf 2010a, p. 126).

Figure 9.1 Model of community development

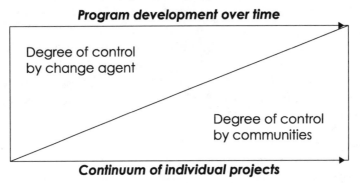

The Model of Community Empowerment shows that communities and organisations that act as 'change agents' in developing work have a varying degree of control of the different individual projects that form part of an overall development program. In the initial stages, change agents are largely in control of project planning and management processes, while the degree of community responsibility is low. In order to change power structures and achieve community empowerment, expert knowledge, skills, responsibilities and ultimately, control need to be transferred step-by-step from the change agent to the empowered communities, who are expected to guide and lead projects in the long term. Time is a critical factor during this process. Looking at AGSEP's work in disadvantaged communities in a developing world context, a complete transfer of ownership may take up to ten years to be sustainable.

In line with their sustainable development strategy, the Marawila community decided to establish an International Sport School in their community that offers sport and tourism courses for local youth. Construction of the International Sport School took almost five years, but the buildings were finally completed in 2011, with lectures starting in September. The aim is to educate children from the region in sport and tourism matters, and do so in a multi-lingual, multi-ethnic context. It is hoped that this purposeful education program will provide the community with qualified and open-minded graduates who can contribute to the local tourism, event and sport sectors in the long run. Funding for the International School was generated from international aid money and private donations, special event projects and other financial and in-kind community contributions.

Networks for innovation

Without reliable local and international networks, the co-operative tourism endeavours of AGSEP and Aquarius Resort could have never been realised; in fact, the significant internal and external barriers would have likely detracted from the success of the integrative sport tourism and development program. Firstly, personal networks are important to establish the initial contact and co-operation between key players in the sport, event and tourism industry, community members, representatives of clubs or associations, and/or government officials. Having influential people on board allows for the sharing of existing networks and the commencement of a multiplier effect. For example, Dr Döring built on existing relationships with other players in the sport business world to arrange sport exchanges between German and Sri Lankan table tennis clubs. Once the first events were successfully staged, more and more people got to know about the program and the Aquarius Resort in Sri Lanka, and consequently decided to take part in future activities. Similarly, Dr Döring's contacts to the government and LTTE sports council have proven beneficial in regards to the quick and reliable handling of visa documents for sport exchanges, and the granting of permissions to enter the northeastern parts of Sri Lanka for negotiations and intercultural sporting events during times of conflict and war.

Secondly, the local tourism network in and around Marawila secures community support and provides a special and authentic Sri Lankan experience to all visitors. While most international sport teams are staying at the Aquarius Resort, many daily activities, outings and performances are provided by the local tourism operators. This arrangement results in a win-win-win situation for the resort, the local businesses and the international tourists: Aquarius Resort can offer authentic Sri Lankan products and services; the local businesses enjoy an increase in tourist demand; and the internationals benefit from local expertise in gaining a truly authentic Sri Lankan experience.

Summary

The innovative and sustainable idea of linking sport event tourism with community development has proven to be beneficial to AGSEP, the Aquarius Resort and local communities and tour operators in post-war Sri Lanka. The sport exchange program has provided more than 5,000 international participants with the opportunity to have a socio-cultural experience in a foreign country, whilst thousands of locals were given the opportunity to participate in peaceful inter-community sport events on the island. In times of difficult socio-political circumstances and civil war in Sri Lanka, AGSEP has continuously attracted international sport tourists to the Aquarius Resort and has given local businesses and communities the chance to benefit both socially and economically. Today, Sri Lankans work for AGSEP, for the International Sport School and in the management of the Aquarius Resort. However, the transition from external to local management has been a long and difficult process, which suggests that we cannot expect disadvantaged communities to take control in a short period of time. This finding has significant implications for project organisers and funding bodies that support development programs in a developing world context. Clearly, long-term strategies for knowledge transfer and local capacity building should go hand in hand with event implementation and project management.

In the case of AGSEP in Sri Lanka, the local, national, international and interethnic networks created over the years form a great part of the program's overall success. In other words, networks were a crucial factor for overcoming internal and external barriers in a country heavily affected by intergroup tensions and warfare. In summary, despite its challenges, AGSEP's innovative community sport event tourism projects have benefited the investors, the tourists and the local Sri Lankan communities, as much as these players have contributed to AGSEP's success over the years.

References

Burnett, C 2006, 'Building Social Capital through an "Active Community Club"'. *International Review for the Sociology of Sport* 41(3-4): 283-294.

Gammanpila, A 2002, 'Thousands pack Vavuniya stadium to witness German footballers', *Daily Mirror Online*, 2 October, www.dailymirror.lk/2002/10/05/sports/1.html.

Gasser, PK, & Levinsen, A 2004, 'Breaking Post-War Ice: Open Fun Football Schools in Bosnia and Herzegovina', *Sport in Society* 7(3): 457-472.

Kidd, B 2008, 'A new social movement: Sport for development and peace', *Sport in Society* 11(4): 370-380.

Schulenkorf, N 2010a, 'The Roles and Responsibilities of a Change Agent in Sport Event Development Projects', *Sport Management Review* 13(2): 118-128.

Schulenkorf, N 2010b, 'Sport events and ethnic reconciliation: Attempting to create social change between Sinhalese, Tamil and Muslim sportspeople in war-torn Sri Lanka', *International Review for the Sociology of Sport* 45(3): 273-294.

Sugden, J 2006, 'Teaching and Playing Sport for Conflict Resolution and Co-Existence in Israel', *International Review for the Sociology of Sport* 41(2): 221-240.

Chapter 10

The Sustainable Tourism Laboratory

Integrating tourism communities

LARRY QUICK

INTRODUCTION

The Blackstone Valley was the birthplace of the industrial revolution in the US. Its network of villages and towns grew rapidly around industrialisation energised by an abundant watershed and other conditions that provided a labor force and access to ports for distribution of finished product (Blackstone River Valley National Heritage Corridor 2006). Initial conditions like this made the Valley a major attraction for industrial growth. However, visit the towns of the Valley today and, like many places, its future is battling through the remnants of the past glories of the industrial age, and the realities of growing 21st century capability. While aspects of its heritage and setting might provide a rich environment for tourism, the Valley struggles under a set of conditions that make sustainable economic and social development problematic. These two factors combine to make tourism both a friend through economic development, and a foe in terms of the community looking to own its own future, outside of tourism.

Tourism is one capability that has its obvious benefits, but, in taking a whole-place or whole-system view, it cannot be developed in isolation from other decisions that affect communities. One factor in these decisions is the disparate socioeconomic makeup of communities: the Valley is home to a large population of immigrants (both documented and undocumented) whose long-term welfare must be taken into account. The river with many heritage buildings along its banks is central to the Blackstone Valley watershed. The river is both a beauty and a beast, and requires long-term understanding as to how it will function in a fast-changing climate, within extreme and volatile weather conditions. The Valley must also be clear on how other global conditions will impact it. The rise in energy costs, the need to switch to other energy sources, food prices and security, the cost of being carbon neutral, the cost of climate change and a state (Rhode Island) in recession are a few of the economic and social pressures that the whole-place view must take into account. In creating a strategy, the Valley and its many stakeholders must make integrated innovation decisions that include conditions that impact the whole, and do not create unintended negative consequences for its parts. For instance, a tourism strategy that created negative synergy for the broader, social, economic and ecological facets of the Valley would be counter-productive to the whole, including tourism itself.

Figure 10.1 Blackstone River Heritage Corridor

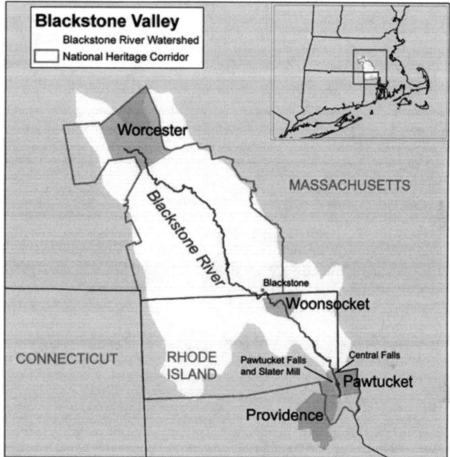

Since 1985, the Blackstone Valley Tourism Council (BVTC) has built its tourism platform on the concept of place-making (not place-taking) (Billington 2006); a commitment to a holistic social, economic, ecological, cultural and built form of development at the local level. In choosing this approach, the BVTC acknowledges that the Blackstone Valley and tourism within the Valley are elements of a larger, whole system, or 'system of systems' that are interdependent and synergistic. If one system fails, it brings down all. The BVTC believes that without this view, the Council and tourism in the Valley will not survive and thrive. This type of thinking is driving the Council to innovate tourism in partnership with the communities they represent, at a deeper level than tourism.

A key innovation of the BVTC is the Sustainable Tourism Laboratory (STL). The STL is a community-based, socially aware teaching and learning network committed to working with city, state and federal governments to positively transform the Blackstone River Valley. The Laboratory concept capitalises on the Valley's implemented sustainable tourism practices and seeks to share them with destinations around the world. Though still in its infancy, the STL is starting to apply complex adaptive systems methods through resilience thinking and a resilient community process as a basis for its theory and practice. In this approach, tourism is seen as one critical driver of community resilience: the ability of a system (community) to absorb destruction and still retain its basic function and structure (Walker & Salt 2007), or the ability of a whole community to transform its capabilities ahead of change, and generate sustainable value for all in the community (Quick 2007).

The Laboratory's purpose is to introduce the concept of planned sustainable tourism to local, regional, state, provincial and worldwide tourism leaders and community stakeholders aiming to develop viable and successful destinations (Billington & Cadoppi 2007). The STL is not a building; it is a place-centered network that will expand its practice of resilience within communities to include tourism-centered communities from across the US. In the Blackstone Valley, it uses local social, economic, ecological, built, natural and historical environments as cases for and demonstrations of tourism, sustainability and resilient communities. By deliberately embracing an open-source process, the STL envisages that as the network grows it will inspire connections with other community nodes, leading to the development of a global network of resilient tourism professionals and practitioners.

Through strategic action, the STL is actively provoking government and the private sector (often seen as barriers to sustainable tourism) to adopt resilient tourism processes, and to approach innovation and development in a way that supports a community's values and enhances its ability to become resilient.

Drivers of innovation

In conventional community development, drivers of innovation are typically those that will either try to maintain a community the way it is (for instance, to sustain a social, economic, cultural, ecological and built form), or change it for the better (to innovate novel and resilient social, economic, cultural, ecological and built forms). A decision as to what to innovate and why is often driven by incrementalism (Dwyer & Edwards 2009) in adaptation to a perceived problem or opportunity, a narrow focus of community, or a single departmental or 'siloed' agenda.

The STL resilient communities approach takes a broad view of innovation and the need to transform communities through three key perspectives: community, embracing complexity and adaptive cycles. A community within the STL connects and operates itself as a 'whole place'. As a resilient community it is a whole, complex system: a network of networks; a 'plexus' (Quick 2007) that only works if key systems are aligned, connected and working in tune with each other. Diverse elements like social, ecological, economic, education, cultural or built environments are understood to be interdependent, and a community understands that intervening in one environment will impact on others.

Places and organisational forms within the STL are subject to a broad scale of local, regional and global conditions that are continuously and discontinuously changing the environment that shapes a community. Hence communities are complex, and to be resilient they must embrace this complexity by continually looking inside and outside to establish an authentic 360-degree view of the conditions that will or may impact them. Through this view, the community can build a shared context that provides a foundation for truly inclusive decision-making across a whole-place and whole-community view, feeding information and giving direction to both tourism and non-tourism related capabilities.

STL communities understand that they are subject to an innate, natural cycle of change that they may either follow or ignore, at their own risk. The notion of an adaptive cycle (Holling 2001) is a highly useful metaphor to understand such changes and to describe the behavior of social, economic and ecological systems through space (geographic scale) and time (history and future planning). The adaptive cycle posits that all systems experience four phases. This understanding is important for policy and management, as each phase provides a different point of leverage for innovation and change.

Figure 10.1 The adaptive cycle within a whole-place view

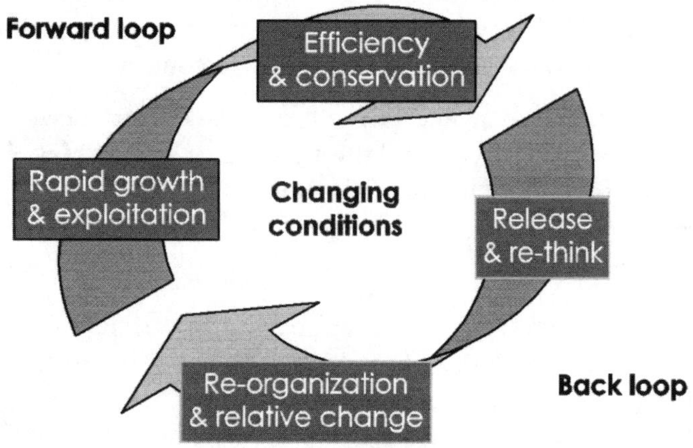

Source: Holling 2001.

Early in the cycle, the system is engaged in a phase of rapid growth and exploitation as an innovation takes hold and new opportunities are created. Within this phase, the role of innovation is to 'trim-tab', or add value, to the originating innovation, and to create momentum for the system to transition to the next phase.

In the efficiency and conservation stage, innovation is used to maintain the state of the system: that is, to keep it in a state of near equilibrium so that maximum returns are drawn from minimum input. All states of the adaptive cycle are inextricably linked to the changing conditions that provide the context and path through the transition of the system. When conditions no longer support the efficiency phase, a new set of conditions drives the system to re-think and release a new and novel form or change of state that will be sustainable within the new conditions. This phase represents the most challenging environment for innovators, as it requires a completely different approach to innovation and innovation leadership that will take a community from a history of certainty into a story of possibility and uncertainty, based on (more than likely) weak signals from conditions that are only understood at an intuitive, non-experiential level.

As the system innovates a new form and begins to balance creativity and structure, it transitions from ideas and possibilities to an organised form that is consistent with change. Innovation at this phase requires an ability to drive toward growth and exploitation, and so the cycle repeats itself. It is possible for the cycle to break down at any phase, but the two states where the system is most vulnerable are the leap of faith between reorganisation and rapid growth, and the move from conservation and efficiency to release and re-think.

A key outcome of the adaptive cycle for the STL is strategic adaptation that creates resilience and resilient communities. The high resilience would mean that the system had a great ability to resist external disturbances and persist, even beyond the point where it is adaptive and creative (Holling 2001, p. 400). Communities achieve this by closely watching the immediate and emergent conditions, and in the context of changing conditions asking: 'is a forward or back loop strategy required?' Given this information, they are in a position to innovate capabilities that align and are adaptive to changes in conditions.

It is the belief of the STL that, like any other social/economic form, tourism is subject to these three perspectives, and if tourism is to be a primary underpinning element of a community, tourism initiatives must be driven by these principles.

Barriers to innovation

In the context of the above types of conditions and the adaptive cycle, the Valley faced decisions of what capabilities to invest in from a forward-loop perspective, and what to let go of to innovate in the back loop. This is a hard decision for communities to make as they are caught between the successes of the past and a distant, risky creative 'product' of the future. However, if the focus is on over-innovating within the efficiency and conservation stage, communities take the risk of holding on to capabilities that only bear value within a past set of conditions. Over-innovation in capabilities that are no longer supported by conditions provides marginal return (if any) and the maximum payback is only ever in the gentle journey to oblivion of managed adaptive decline (MAD). Very well-managed adaptive decline has been an abundant element of the Valley's past 'growth strategy'. This must now change: emergent conditions demand that it quickly drives innovation that responds to the realities of the 21st century, and lets go of elements of a 20th century that is long gone.

The innovation challenge for tourism in the Blackstone Valley is addressed through the following question: Considering that whole place environment is characterised by a broad raft of very necessary social, economic, ecological, cultural and built environment reforms, what role does tourism play in the Blackstone Valley of the 21st century?

From an STL perspective, the issue of barriers to innovation revolved less around the forces that stop innovation, and more around the capabilities and commitment to innovation that have the potential to generate a resilient future. The initial tasks of creating a whole-place view, an intimate understanding of conditions and a strategic use of the adaptive cycle are all initial barriers to resilient innovation. Municipalities, organisations and innovators generally tend to take a different view of change and innovation to that taken by those committed to resilience and resilient communities. This situation represents an innovation challenge for innovators themselves as they have to release and rethink their approach to innovation and to reorganise their thinking and the processes they use. Like all resilient innovations, if the present state has provided strong efficiencies and rewards, change is highly problematic and more than likely will not happen without a crisis in conditions, where conditions are such that they force the system into a new state that is far from the original state being held onto.

Processes for innovation

A strategy to plan, develop and promote tourism in the Blackstone Valley began with the incorporation of the not-for-profit Blackstone Valley Tourism Council and the establishment of the Valley National Heritage Corridor (VNHC) in 1986. Blackstone River Valley National Heritage Corridor (BRVNHCC) represents 24 communities, some 400,000 acres and over 500,000 people. BRVNHCC was formed to support, protect and celebrate the birthplace of the American Industrial Revolution. The BRVNHC was established as a bi-state, federally-appointed commission of local and state representatives to help preserve and interpret the unique resources and qualities that made the Blackstone Valley significant both to the nation and to its residents. The BRVNHC was born out of an innovative idea to enlist the National Park Service in a partnership dedicated to helping states and localities conserve their special regions: those places where historical and natural characteristics had left their mark on American history. At the time, this was an ambitious experiment; no one knew whether it would work or not.

Supported by the STL, the approach was based on thinking about regional places. Rather than conceiving Blackstone Valley as a set of self-contained independent municipalities divided by political boundaries, residents were asked to envision the Valley as a regional entity: as an interdependent place linked by a common set of economic, natural and cultural resources. Despite some skepticism, the Tourism Council initiated an innovative tourism development vision. Much to the surprise of many businesses and public officials, tourism development in the Valley began to attract visitors. Comprehensive planning continued in 1988, as the National Heritage Corridor adopted strategies of sustainable tourism development, applied by the Tourism Council, as a way to accomplish some of the objectives defined in its plan.

The STL encouraged residents and businesses to act responsibly and to prioritise a long-term return on investment over short-term economic benefits, which could support harmful and wasteful land use. Building a sense of social responsibility among residents was essential in order to regenerate the Valley. The community had to understand that the Blackstone River could be reborn. Community leaders have attracted hundreds of corporations and local residents to work on Blackstone River cleanup projects each year (Blackstone River Valley National Heritage Corridor 2006; Billington & Manheim 2002; Billington 2004).

In 1992, the Blackstone Valley Tourism Council created the Regional Comprehensive Tourism Development Plan for Rhode Island's Blackstone Valley, which was consistent with other state-mandated plans for economic development, low-income housing, heritage preservation and industrial development in the Blackstone Valley. In respect to tourism planning, Patrick Kennedy, US Congressman, stated, 'the Blackstone Valley Tourism Council has worked to inspire private and public investment, and renewed sense of pride in the Blackstone Valley' (personal communication, April 16, 2006).

As a result of co-operation, collaboration and extensive planning, over the past two decades the Blackstone Valley Tourism Council has overseen the emergence of the region as a significant destination for both heritage and nature-based tourism. Blackstone Valley Corridor partners see the Valley as many interconnected systems which make up the whole. From this broad-based systems understanding, the partners work together on three key areas of a sustainable Blackstone Valley:

- a sustainable environment;
- a sustainable economy; and
- a sustainable place (land use, transportation, built form, and preservation of culture and history).

Networks for innovation

The STL and its approach to resilient tourism thrive on its ability to network, share information, work collaboratively and join together to operate individually and as a whole. Imperative for this network is the STL network's ability to understand conditions, create a shared context for decision-making, appropriately connect their capabilities and execute catalytic actions that will benefit the whole. In doing so, two outcomes are achieved. The community employs an open platform innovation system (OPIS).

The STL understands that innovation systems are a critical element of resilience, and that to achieve optimal innovation in today's highly connected world requires an openness that attracts and leverages all manner of entrepreneurship and collaborative effort. Hence, the platform may be owned by a community, but is also open to partners to allow interested parties to align with its common cause. Valley partners continue to work together to create a Corridor-wide Sustainability Strategy through:

- broad and diverse involvement of citizens;
- the creation of a collective vision for the future;
- the development of principles of sustainability,
- an inventory of existing assets and resources and additional assets that would benefit the community;
- clear, measurable goals;
- the development of community indicators to evaluate progress;
- open and transparent communication;
- key catalytic projects to engage citizens;
- early, visible results; and
- celebration of success.

The community is the message and the medium. STL communities are deeply conversational and interact through a combination of media forms. They do not rely on 'the media' for news, to communicate with each other, or to set the agenda: they are the agenda. Social networks drive an 'organic narrative' that spells out clearly what the STL community is and what it is up to.

Over the past ten years, the STL has focused its attention on the continuation of a dynamic plan to provide guidance of the basic principles while recognizing the need to grow and address changing circumstances. To balance new partnerships with existing commitments, the BRVNHC management plans have focused on four objectives: tell the story of the American industrial revolution; preserve and enhance valley communities; balance conservation and growth; and promote recovery of the river for swimming and fishing by 2015.

Summary

The STL's mission was informed by significant and critical sustainable tourism development issues. The Laboratory fulfills this mission by designing and presenting a series of robust symposiums, conferences, and programs to link the Laboratory's work to the local and global arenas (Billington, Carter & Kayamba 2007). The critical and immediate need to pursue sustainability strategies is well documented and broadcast throughout the world. The idea of a sustainable future is consistent not only with how the STL works within the natural environment, but also with how its social, economic and built systems holistically comply with sustainable change. The STL has long been committed to sustainable growth; a key underlying principle it follows is that in planning and innovating for sustainability, there is a global need to change processes and practices that may have served tourism in the past, but are not appropriate for the future.

The STL has applied the United Nations Environmental Programme (2005) and World Tourism Organization (2004) principles to become a sustainable visitor destination. The Valley has preserved its environment, respected the sociocultural authenticity of the local communities, and provided economic growth to all stakeholders. Leadership, creativity, collaboration, commitment and social accountability from all sectors of the community have led the Valley to find its direction, follow its vision and share it with others along the way (Billington & Manheim 2002).

References

Billington, RD 1999, 'Building bridges of peace, culture & prosperity through sustainable tourism', in RW Blanchard & GD Praetzel (eds), *Third Global Conference - International Institute for Peace through Tourism. Regeneration of an industrial landscape through tourism – The Blackstone River Valley of New England*, Niagara University, New York: 74.

Billington, RD 2004, 'Federal leverage attracts private investment at US heritage sites: A case study', *International Journal of Heritage Studies* 10(4): 349-359.

Billington, RD & Manheim, P 2002, 'Tourism in Asia: Development, Marketing, and Sustainability', in K Chon, VCS Heung & KKF Wong (eds), *Fifth Biennial Conference, Creating sustainable tourism development - The Blackstone Valley National Heritage Corridor - America's First Industrialized Valley: the role of leadership - Creativity, cooperation and commitment*, School of Hotel and Tourism Management, Hong Kong: 25-33.

Billington, RD & Cadoppi, V 2007, 'Stakeholder Involvement, Culture and Accountability in the Blackstone Valley: A Work in Progress', in J Liburd & A Hergesell (eds), *Conference proceedings of the BEST EN Think Tank VI Corporate Social Responsibility for Sustainable Tourism*, 13-16 June 2006, Girona, Spain, University of Western Sydney, Sydney, Australia.

Blackstone Valley Tourism Council 1992, *Blackstone River Valley Rhode Island: Regional comprehensive tourism plan 1992 for the communities of Pawtucket, Cumberland, Central Falls, Woonsocket, North Smithfield, Glocester, Burrillville, Lincoln and Smithfield*, Author, Pawtucket, RI.

Holling, CS 2001, 'Understanding the Complexity of Economic, Ecological, and Social Systems', *Ecosystems* 4: 390–405.

National Park Service Blackstone River Heritage Corridor, accessed 29 April 2012, www.nps.gov/blac/index.htm.

United Nations Environment Programme & World Tourism Organization 2005, *Making tourism more sustainable: A guide for policy makers*, Authors, Paris, France and Madrid, Spain.

World Tourism Organization 2004, *Sustainable development of tourism: Conceptual definition*, accessed 10 February 2006, www.world-tourism.org/frameset/frame_sustainable.html.

Chapter 11

Wenhai Ecolodge
Community-based innovations for sustainability

GINGER SMITH AND JIAYI DU

INTRODUCTION

The case of Wenhai Ecolodge in northwest Yunnan, China, may be regarded as a cogent example of current and future successful development of community-based tourism innovations for sustainable destination management in China. Yunnan Province is one of the most ethnically, geographically, and biologically diverse places in China. Approximately three million people live in Yunnan Province, including 13 of China's 55 ethnic minorities, making it a culturally diverse and uniquely attractive tourism destination. In 2006, Yunnan Province's tourism revenue reached $6.2b and accounted for 12.5% of the GDP. The northwestern portion of Yunnan is famous for its rural villages, and the Old Town of Lijiang is also a UNESCO World Heritage Site.

Wenhai Ecolodge is a community-operated retreat in Northwest Yunnan run by a local co-operative of 56 households from upper Wenhai village with support from the United States (US) based Nature Conservancy. This lodge is nestled in a valley at approximately 10,000 feet above sea level and about 15 miles from Lijiang, one of China's loveliest cities. There are 12 newly renovated and nicely appointed rooms in the lodge, with room rates starting at US$12 per day. Every household purchased shares and contributed start-up financing through a loan to the Ecolodge. The Ecolodge uses sustainable energy systems, including biogas and solar panels, to decrease the impact on the surrounding resources by reducing or eliminating the dependence on fossil fuels as an energy source. It also has a small library with information and books about the cultural and natural resources of

Wenhai. Ten percent of the lodge's profits go to a conservation and community development fund that supports projects around Wenhai Lake. In 2003, Wenhai was named one of the World's Ten Best Ecolodges by Outside Magazine. Wenhai also co-operates with Northwest Yunnan Ecotourism Association, whose goals are to support environmental protection, preserve the area's diverse cultural heritage, and contribute to community development.

Map 11.1 Northwest Yunnan

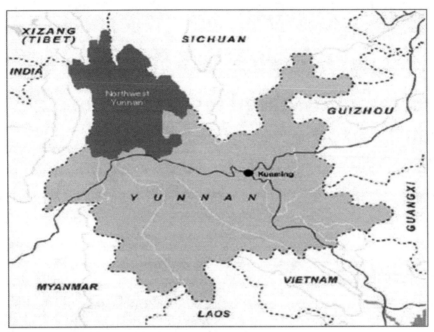

Drivers of innovation

Through employment with community-based ecotourism companies, local villagers are able to earn much-needed tourism-generated revenues that replace income earned through destructive practices such as illegal game hunting/poaching, logging/clear cutting for fuel/charcoal-making and over-fishing for food supplies. Biogas, solar panels and, in some cases, wind or hydropower help to reduce the drain on natural resources that tourism can bring to a community. Furthermore, local residents who open their own guesthouses are proactively embracing these kinds of sustainable energy solutions.

Managers and employees of companies are local community members who benefit directly through skills training in such areas as nature guiding, hospitality services and business management. Some of the local young people learn English and enhance their language skills by working as travel and tourism guides. These activities contribute to employment and retention of human resources in the local tourism-related industries. Additionally, more indigenous families are reconstructing their houses, opening bed-and-breakfast establishments and small hotels to accommodate tourists. Most agreed that their traditional lifestyles are not significantly or negatively changed, and have increased their family incomes.

Companies are owned and managed by local community members, which enables the community to direct and influence the development of tourism in their area. Since the company is community-owned, the local residents retain most of the income and have the greatest influence on the future development of the sustainable tourism destination management project in their community (in this case, the Wenhai Ecolodge resort community).

By observing visitors' interest in and enthusiasm for Chinese local culture, the value of their cultural heritage has also increased among community members. Family traditions have passed from generation to generation because of their sustainable tourism destination management practices and the growing interest worldwide of intangible cultural heritage.

Barriers to innovation

There remain numerous internal and external barriers to successful implementation of Northwest Yunnan's sustainable tourism management. First, tourism employers and tourists have multiple misconceptions of the new-found tourism industry. The tourism industry was historically regarded as a non-polluting ('smoke-free') industry in China, especially in early development stages; therefore, many tourist sites lack the early implementation of laws and regulations to control the pollution and environmental degradation that can be caused by the tourism industry. Compared with other industries, the tourism industry in some respects requires less initial investment and produces higher immediate profitability. Tourism resources are misperceived as inexhaustible and able to be utilised perpetually. These kinds of misunderstandings have led to increasing investment in tourism products without the implementation of appropriate sustainable planning, innovation and development measures. Furthermore, sustainable tourism becomes a grandly applied and often misused term in many cases. Consequently, unmanaged tourism development too often occurs in the name of sustainable tourism.

When industry employees and tourists do not have a clear understanding of the drivers and reasons for innovation in the industry, misguided policies and decision-making can often harm the industry. A primary reason behind this demise is the lack of professional education and training of all constituents in the industry. Many employees in the tourism industry do not have a proper education background or training experience. More than half the employees do not have any experience or professional skills whatsoever when they begin their careers in the tourism industry. Some tourists, too, fail to recognise their responsibilities to protect the environment, and thoughtlessly leave litter behind during their trip.

From the administrative perspective, proper industry management systems are lacking in China for many reasons. Tourism resources are owned and managed by the government in China; however, government decision-makers are ill-informed in relation to sustainable tourism. Significant negative ecological effects on Yunnan's tourism resources occurred because of the government dam project at

Tiger Leaping Gorge. Local government is interested in promoting the tourism industry to gain economic benefits, but offers little support in areas such as sustainable tourism project management. Profitability is frequently regarded as one of the most important measures of government investment. Market mechanisms in China are in an early stage, and there is a lack of relevant laws and policies with respect to tourism that are binding.

Processes for innovations

The model of donating a minimum percentage of net profits (in this case 10%) to a conservation and community development fund has proved successful for providing financial support for further community development, innovation and conservation projects in local areas. To ensure that visitor activities do not have any significant negative impact on the resources and local communities in the area, visitor management systems are currently being established. These include:

- zoning to control ecologically and culturally sensitive areas and the number of tourists permitted to visit them;
- codes of conduct for ecotourists and tour operators;
- village ecotourism resource monitoring teams; and
- national and local enforcement policies and regulation mechanisms.

A community vision has been developed by community members to identify cultural traditions that they wish to preserve. With these guidelines in place, the impact of tourism on traditional customs can be measured and monitored, and controls can be established if it is determined that tourism is having a negative effect on the local cultures.

Networks for innovation

Networks play an important role in the innovation of sustainable tourism. A number of organisations and associations have emerged to assist communities and villages in China to promote sustainable tourism. The Northwest Yunnan Ecotourism Association is a local organisation sponsored by the US-based Nature Conservancy. The Ecotourism Association was developed to introduce tourists to unique ecotourism opportunities around Lijiang and beyond. By developing and promoting ecotourism in Northwest Yunnan, the Association's goal is to support environmental protection, preserve the area's diverse cultural heritage and contribute to community development through job creation.

In the case of Wenhai Lodge, a management committee, comprising non-government organisations (NGOs), government, and community representatives, oversees and approves all projects initiated with the community development. A portion of profits generated through the tourist itineraries in the local community goes to funding community development projects, such as micro-hydroelectricity, irrigation, education and health services. Importantly, community members are not only heard but also determine what types of projects should be implemented.

Summary

The 'real' dilemma or opportunity of sustainable tourism destination management in China is hard to ascertain because it is still early in the innovation evaluation process. It is difficult, therefore, to state with certainty that the Wenhai Ecolodge, as a pilot model for other emerging ecolodges, is moving forward in the facilitation of sustainable tourism in the Northwest Yunnan region, let alone in China more generally. The Northwest Yunnan Ecotourism Association at Wenhai can provide lessons, for example, for the Wulingyuan Nature Reserve and other regions in China on both internal and external barrier reduction and experiences in both the costs and benefits of networks for innovation in sustainable tourism destination management.

First, however, the relationship between protection, tourism and people's livelihood should be managed appropriately. The protection of heritage resources is a prerequisite for the sustainable development of tourism and a better quality of life for the people in host communities. As mentioned above, the higher the values local residents place on their own economic, socio-cultural and environmental heritage, the stronger their commitment to protect and preserve these cultural heritage values and share them with visitors from other parts of China and the world.

Second, the involvement of local communities and networks are key to sustainable tourism destination management in China from a long-term perspective. When individuals are engaged collectively and co-operatively in innovation networks as in the case of the Wenhai Ecolodge project, successful sustainable destination management can be facilitated. The local community is comprised of people who personally and professionally best understand the interplay between public, private, and non-profit tourism organisations, tourism's natural, human and economic resources, and cultural values as drivers for innovation for sustainable tourism in China.

References

Northwest Yunnan Ecotourism Association, accessed 20 December 2007, www.northwestyunnan.com.

Wulingyuan map, accessed 14 December 2007, www.wulingyuan.com/map/wulingyuanmap.html.

Yan, Xiaorong & Yan, F 2006, 'Experience and lessons from tourism exploitation inWulingyuan world natural heritage', *Ecological Economy* 2: 424-432.

Yang, M & Zhou, G 2005, 'Study on effective measures of environmental protection for sustainable development of tourism industry in the world heritage Wulingyuan', *Ecological Economy* 1(2): 83-88.

Zhong, L, Deng, J & Xiang, B (in press), *Tourism development and the tourism area life-cycle model: A case study of Zhangjiajie National Forest Park, China*, corrected proof, Tourism Management.

Chapter 12

Cross-case analysis
New insights into innovation

JACK CARLSEN AND JANNE J LIBURD

INTRODUCTION

Cross-case analysis is a means of grouping together common responses to interviews and analysing different perspectives on central issues (Patton 1990; Getz *et al.* 2004). Cross-case analysis is based on a structured case for each unit studied; responses are then grouped together according to the key questions listed in the introduction and the key themes and sub-themes found in the relevant literature. In this way, the convergent and divergent issues that emerge in each case study are integrated within a descriptive analytical framework that provides the basis for comparison and contrast.

In this chapter, cross-case analysis provides a summary of common, convergent outcomes and insights associated with the drivers, barriers and processes of sustainable tourism innovation and the role of networks for innovation. Common themes to each of the case studies provide a means of cross-referencing case studies to the relevant themes that have emerged. As with any qualitative, descriptive research, it is necessary to validate the thematic framework and case study findings and identify the contribution to knowledge that is made through the research. Whilst individual case studies by their nature have limited generalisability, the themes and sub-themes that they capture can be related to the wider body of theory and practical knowledge on innovation for sustainable tourism. Cross-case analysis is used to highlight the main themes in innovation for sustainable tourism, as well as to identify new and emergent issues that may not have been identified in the literature. This analytical component of case study research should provide readers with an overview and insight into extant and new themes in networks, innovation and sustainable tourism.

Drivers of innovation

Bergin-Seers, Breen and Frew (2008) found eight determinants or indicators of innovative capacity that cover a number of management capabilities and behaviours:

- competent management;
- external relationship management;
- management of information;
- recognition of employees;
- acknowledgement of customer relations;
- market knowledge;
- implementation of a systematic new product development process; and
- awareness of barriers.

These capabilities are embedded in the case studies in this volume and are all determinants or drivers of innovation to a greater or lesser extent (Table 12.1).

It is evident from cross-case analysis that external relationship management and awareness of barriers are the main pre-requisites to innovation for sustainable tourism. External relationships with suppliers, customers, community groups and government agencies proved to be critical to driving innovation in seven of the ten cases. The formation of innovation networks was integral to the formation and management of external relations in all cases and none of the innovations took place independently or in isolation, in accordance with Lundvall (2005).

An awareness of the internal and external barriers to innovation is also important in six of the cases, and overcoming resistance to change in land use, consumer habits, operating procedures, community attitudes, entrenched social attitudes and a lack of understanding and communication became the drivers of innovation in the cases identified in Table 12.1.

Two additional drivers emerged from the cross-case analysis: the social, economic, cultural and environmental values held by managers; and the degree of commitment to innovation in their organisation. In seven of the cases, the values of the individuals and organisations are clearly articulated and management commitment to innovation is demonstrated. For example, Scandic Hotels' environmental awareness and associated values were first enunciated in the Brundtland Report in 1987, and then captured in the Natural Step principles of 'New Scandic' which aimed to 'to lead the way and work continuously to promote both a reduction in our environmental impacts and a better environment' (Nattrass & Altomare 1999; Scandic 2003). There are social values underpinning Scandic's sustainability also: the concept of Omtanke, meaning 'caring for our guests and each other while caring for the environment and the society around us' (Scandic 2007); the belief that it is 'in everybody's right to be treated equally, feel safe and be well taken care of [so called Nordic common sense]'; and the aim to 'offer easy and accessible travel for all' (Scandic 2007). This ethical behaviour is also found in the case study of Xanterra, who believed that an EMS program was 'the right thing to do'. Clearly, this makes good business practice, so it fits well with corporate strategy and economic sustainability and provides a rationale for management to commit to the sometimes costly and risky innovation process.

The AGSEP case demonstrates the social values of the Founder and CEO, Dr Dietmar Döring, in seeking to address the ongoing political and civil conflict in Sri Lanka by using social sporting events as peaceful means of resolving ethnic and cultural differences and fostering unity and understanding between the three main ethnic groups. Social stability is a pre-requisite to economic development, so these values have direct implications for social as well as economic sustainability. For the AGSEP, creating harmonious lived experiences is central to the building, bridging and bonding of conflicting communities.

Table 12.1 Drivers of innovation and relevant cases

Determinant	Relevant case(s)
Competent and committed management	Scandic Hotels, Xanterra LLC, AGSEP, EDDA
External relationship management	Ecocean, Scandic Hotels, Xanterra LLC, Diablo Trust, AGSEP, Blackstone Valley STL, Wenhai Ecolodge
Management of information	Ecocean, Xanterra LLC, Blackstone Valley STL
Recognition of employees	Scandic Hotels, EDDA
Acknowledgement of customer relations	Scandic Hotels, EDDA, Wenhai Ecolodge
Implementation of a new systematic product development process	Tasting Arizona, EDDA
Awareness of barriers	Diablo Trust, Tasting Arizona, Scandic Hotels, AGSEP, Brenu Beach Resort, EDDA, Blackstone Valley STL
Values held by management	Scandic Hotels, Xanterra LLC, AG.S.E.P., EDDA, Brenu Beach Resort, Blackstone Valley STL, Wenhai Ecolodge
Management commitment to innovation	Scandic Hotels, Ecocean, Xanterra LLC, Diablo Trust, Tasting Arizona, EDDA, Blackstone Valley STL

Conserving culture and tradition can be just as important as conserving nature in the drive to innovate for sustainable tourism: this was true in the cases of Scandic, EDDA, Brenu Beach Resort, Diablo Trust, Blackstone Valley STL and Wenhai Ecolodge. The cultural values of lived experiences and unique memories can be realised in the way that they are expected by visitors and delivered by tourism operators and staff. For example, the Wenhai Ecolodge has introduced zoning to control ecologically and culturally sensitive areas and the number of tourists permitted to visit them; codes of conduct for ecotourists and tour operators; village ecotourism resource monitoring teams; and national and local enforcement policies and regulation mechanisms. Another perspective is added by the EDDA case, which recognises that the skilled and competent staff in the Danish attractions sector play a crucial role in creating those sought-after experiences. Hence, innovation in staff training, creation of networks and innovative management is a key to delivering memorable experiences. Of all the drivers of innovation for sustainable tourism businesses and the associated cultural values that underpin them, the most powerful is survival. The power of the human spirit and ability to adapt in the most challenging and confronting circumstances with whatever resources are available is an abiding characteristic of innovation. It is evident in the case study of the female entrepreneur, dubbed Aunty Aggie, of the Brenu Beach Resort region in Ghana. Likewise, the Metzger and Prosser families were motivated by the desire to maintain their cattle ranching traditions and lifestyle so that future generations can experience the 'wild west', as portrayed in the past.

Conservation values come to the fore in the case of Ecocean, where the drive and commitment of Dr Brad Norman to conserve the threatened whale shark and generate public awareness of its status and vulnerability became his passion. Innovation in the collection and management of whale shark identification, information data and mapping of their migration was the key to achieving conservation. Conservation values were also evident in the case of Diablo Trust, Xanterra LLC and Tasting Arizona. Conserving habitat and species was not only important to these organisations, but also to the lifestyle and future of those that live on the land or visit places of natural and cultural significance. Acknowledging locals as users and stakeholders secures local accessibility to valued environments (Cohen 2002). It also enables preservation of cultural values and promotes intergenerational equity by making such principles and values explicit while acknowledging that all cultures are subject to change over time.

Barriers to innovation

Breen *et al.* (2006) found that the main barriers challenging the ability of tourist parks to be innovative included both internal and external factors. These could be broadly classified as internal knowledge, financial, human resources, business barriers and external legislative/political, environmental, social, technological barriers. These are evident in each of the case studies (Table 12.2).

Scandic Hotel's main internal barrier was a lack of environmental awareness by their staff. Consequently, the implementation of an environmental policy had to include specific actions for each hotel in the chain and each team member. This made implementation an incremental process, starting with altering the practices of employees and culminating in the phased introduction of technical solutions in co-operation with suppliers. Incremental innovation is a necessary approach for overcoming barriers to innovation; uncertainty in internal and external operating environments will often introduce barriers at all stages in the innovation process.

These uncertainties were found in a number of cases and can be related to the financial, operational, legal or technical aspects (Table 12.2) of the actions undertaken on the path to innovation. In all cases, a creative and determined solution needed to be applied to realise the goals of the innovation.

Social barriers were also present in some cases, with suspicion and skepticism amongst resident and business communities emerging in a number of cases (Table 12.2). Change in society is always challenging and confronting for those that have embedded social norms and practices, so those that seek to innovate can expect to encounter social barriers ranging from community resistance to political intervention at some point in the innovation process. Understanding and working through the uncertainties and concerns amongst communities that can accompany any form of change, especially in the highly visible and critical area of tourism is one of the key requirements for those seeking to move towards sustainability through innovation. This is clearly illustrated in the case of the Blackstone Valley STL, where decision-makers and community stakeholders are engaged in learning and managing one of America's first industrialised and polluted landscapes for a sustainable tourism future.

Table 12.2 Internal and external barriers to innovation and relevant cases

Internal barriers	Relevant case(s)
Knowledge	Scandic Hotels, Ecocean, Blackstone Valley STL, EDDA, Wenhai Ecolodge
Financial	Ecocean, Xanterra LLC, Scandic Hotels, Brenu Beach Resort
Human resources	Scandic Hotels, EDDA, Diablo Trust
Business	Tasting Arizona, Diablo Trust, Xanterra LLC, Scandic Hotels
External barriers	**Relevant case(s)**
Legislative/political	Diablo Trust, Scandic Hotels, AGSEP, Brenu Beach Resort
Environmental	Diablo Trust, Wenhai Ecolodge
Social	Ecocean, AGSEP, Brenu Beach Resort
Technological	Ecocean

Processes for innovation

Schaper and Volery (2007) found that most innovation processes are incremental, as opposed to disruptive, revolutionary innovations, which may be underpinned by cultural practices and values. In some cases, innovation processes can be rapidly implemented, produce immediate gains and customer loyalty, and involve an adaptation of new technology. Table 12.3 summarises these innovation processes and relevant case study examples.

Steady improvement in operating procedures, procurement, environmental management, cultural relations, knowledge creation and dissemination were evident in six of the cases. For example, in a staged process Scandic Hotels first established the core values and communicated those by then engaging employees to implement these. Next, resource use was monitored and reduction in energy use and purchase of products with lower environmental impacts was pursued. The opportunity to adopt new standards in design was introduced during the refurbishment and retrofitting of hotel rooms and facilities. Scandic then reviewed its role in wider society by looking at the specific needs of individuals, addressing accessibility, appointing a disability co-ordinator and adopting standards in accessibility. Finally, Scandic engaged in a communication exercise to inform their customers and the wider Scandinavian society of their improvements and innovations in sustainability. Similarly, Xanterra LLC went about systematically implementing environmental managements systems and procurement programs designed specifically to achieve specific and measureable standards and targets by 2015, with annual monitoring of their environmental performance central to that process.

Table 12.3 Innovation processes and relevant cases

Process	Relevant case(s)
Steady improvement	Scandic Hotels, Xanterra LLC, AGSEP, EDDA, Blackstone Valley STL
Based on cultural practices and values	Diablo Trust, AGSEP, Brenu Beach Resort, Wenhai Ecolodge, Blackstone Valley STL
Rapid implementation	Ecocean
Produce immediate gains	Ecocean, Xanterra LLC
Produce customer loyalty	Tasting Arizona, Scandic Hotels, Xanterra LLC, AGSEP
Adaptation of existing technology	Scandic, Ecocean, Xanterra LLC, Blackstone Valley STL

Cultural practices and values are also integral to most innovations: their incorporation into the innovation process ensures that they are sustained rather than lost in transition. Hence, the Diablo Trust married the conservation efforts with their existing cattle ranching traditions to rehabilitate degraded land and rejuvenate grassland for native animals as well as cattle. Traditional food cultures were conserved in both the Brenu Beach Resort and Tasting Arizona case studies. Cultural understanding between previously ethnically divided groups in Sri Lanka was facilitated through the social sporting organisation AGSEP. The Wenhai Ecolodge has encouraged greater awareness and led to a deeper appreciation of the culture and traditions practiced by the local community in which it operates, in addition to conserving the natural resources upon which ecotourism depends.

When technology is adapted in the innovation process, rapid implementation and improvement is facilitated. This was the case when Ecocean was able to access NASA Space technology as a means of electronically tagging and identifying the magnificent and mysterious whale shark that is the core attraction for marine tourism destinations such as Ningaloo Reef, Western Australia. Technology was also an important component of the innovation process in the cases of Xanterra LLC and Blackstone Valley STL, providing for improvements to management and production processes.

Networks for innovation

In all of the cases, networks were found to be the drivers for innovation and the way to address barriers; they were critical to the process of innovation. Indeed, a new network of actors was the innovation, and ongoing innovation was mainly aimed at expansion of the network to support the implementation and ideals of the original people who developed the ideas. Hence, socio-cultural support networks include many different groups in society, including:

- agricultural, native, educational and scientific groups in the case of Tasting Arizona, Diablo Trust and Wenhai Ecolodge;
- international and local sporting groups in the case of AGSEP; and
- knowledge/learning networks were formed around innovation in the case of Scandic Hotels, EDDA Brenu Beach Resort, AGSEP and, most notably, Ecocean.

Bridging such networks can link different repositories of knowledge and potentially enable the transition to sustainable tourism development (Liburd 2010). Customer and supplier networks were found to be important in all cases, especially Xanterra LLC. Diffusion networks involving suppliers and employees were important in the cases of Scandic Hotels and Xanterra LLC, and local sports associations and tourism businesses were important for AGSEP.

Table 12.4 Innovation networks and relevant cases

Network type	Relevant case(s)
Socio-cultural network	Tasting Arizona, Diablo Trust, AGSEP, Brenu Beach Resort, Blackstone Valley STL, Wenhai Ecolodge
Knowledge/learning network	Scandic Hotels, Ecocean, Brenu Beach Resort, AGSEP, EDDA, Blackstone Valley STL
Management network	Xanterra LLC, Scandic Hotels
Customer/supplier network	Scandic Hotels, Xanterra LLC.
Diffusion network	Scandic Hotels, AGSEP Blackstone Valley STL, Wenhai Ecolodge

Summary

This set of case studies has set out a way in which to structure, describe and analyse the organisations and destinations that are seeking to innovate for sustainable tourism. The overall aims were to provide an avenue for critical thought and debate and to stimulate ideas that can generate discussion and understanding of the nature of innovation for sustainable tourism. During this process, it is equally as important to determine the questions that remain unanswered and the issues that remain unresolved, as it is to identify further research into innovations that can contribute to sustainable tourism in the future. Innovations for sustainable tourism must be based on philosophical reflection upon desired presents and futures and on equitable participation in order to provide a direct contribution to sustainable world making.

Chapter 13 provides researchers and scholars with a set of questions and observations of the context, nature and impact of the innovation in each case and poses a series of possible dilemmas that have and could continue to confront the organisations and individuals described in these case studies. Networks were found to be central to innovation for sustainable tourism in providing the driving values and commitment, overcoming known internal and external barriers and facilitating processes of knowledge creation and dissemination (Hjalager 1996, 2010; Lynch & Morrison, 2007; Laing *et al.* 2008).

Innovation for sustainable tourism is evolving and the networks that support innovation are expanding to accommodate this transition. The internet and the potential to stimulate discussion and ideas and disseminate knowledge through user created content provides the perfect platform for continuous growth of all sorts of networks — social, cultural, managerial, customer, supplier, knowledge and diffusion — that can accelerate the development of innovation and transformation of tourism organisations and destinations to sustainability.

References

Bergin-Seers, S, Breen, JP & Frew, EA 2008, 'The Determinants and Barriers Affecting Innovation Management in Small and Medium Tourism Enterprises (SMTEs) in the Tourist Park Sector', *Tourism Recreation Research* 33(3): 245-253.

Breen, J, Bergin-Seers, S, Roberts, L, Frew, E & Carlsen, J 2006, *Innovation and Change Management for Small and Medium Tourism Enterprises in the Tourist Park Sector*, Sustainable Tourism CRC, Griffith University, Gold Coast.

Cohen, E 2002, 'Authenticity, equity and sustainability in tourism', *Journal of Sustainable Tourism* 10(4): 267-276.

Getz, D, Carlsen, J & Morrison, A 2004, *The Family Business in Tourism and Hospitality*, CABI Publishing, Wallingford.

Laing, J, Wegner, A, Moore, S, Weiler, B, Pfueller, S, Lee, D, Macbeth, J, Croy, G & Lockwood, M 2008, *Developing effective partnerships for facilitating sustainable protected area tourism: Literature review*, Sustainable Tourism CRC, Gold Coast.

Liburd, JJ 2010, 'Sustainable Tourism Development', in JJ Liburd & D Edwards (eds,) *Understanding the Sustainable Development of Tourism*, Goodfellow Publishers: 1-18.

Chapter 13

Learning from case studies

PADDY FORDE

INTRODUCTION

Case studies that describe particular experiences and innovation processes provide insight into local dilemmas and ignite reflection that offers valuable learning at multiple levels. Scholars search case studies to find leads that improve theory. Practitioners appreciate that peer experience can inform or improve personal practice. Students enjoy thinking about how they would have tackled the situation. Therefore, these cases are expected to be utilised by readers in manners that meet their personal needs. Reader variety posed a problem for the editors when presentation and summarisation was considered. For example, structuring cases into a specific format that assisted one type of reader (i.e. students) would inconvenience other readers. As the cases were written by practitioners, their peers are expected to find them useful. Researchers may require more detail and this could be obtained upon request to case authors. Case notes have been provided to assist students looking for ideas on how to enhance their reflection.

These case notes are expected to be particularly useful to students and teaching staff, but they also provide convenient case synopses for other readers. Distilling the context, innovation, drivers, barriers, processes and networks into a few concise sentences naturally encourages cross-case comparison and consequently a focus upon case themes. In addition, a number of suggested dilemmas have been included. Dilemmas remind us that the cases represent snapshots of real situations that will address continuing challenges. Case studies do not merely provide descriptions of experiences and achievements. They also stimulate us to reflect on how we might have tackled a particular situation or to imagine how we would go forward, if we were in that predicament. This reflection is the unique attraction of case studies; dilemmas are a tool that can facilitate that reflection. The dilemmas suggested in these case notes are intended to motivate your thinking:

however, we recognise that reader perspective could easily suggest other interesting dilemmas.

Scandic, Scandinavia

Context

Scandic is one of the largest hotel operators in Scandinavia with more than 130 hotels. It is an independent company that was previously owned by an international hotel chain and the present owners are seeking to expand in Europe.

Declared innovation

A corporate environmental policy and program was implemented, together with action plans for individual hotels.

Influence on sustainability

Scandic reduced energy and water consumption by responsible operation. It encouraged thinking about sustainability by using Omtanke, meaning 'caring for our guests and each other while caring for the environment and the society around us'.

Implementation drivers

Changes in market characteristics caused Scandic to seek a new perspective that could underwrite a differentiated position within the international hotel industry. A strong brand was needed that employees and guests could identify with and that would provide short-term operational gains.

Barriers to achievement

There was lack of knowledge and environmental awareness amongst team members. Having to include external organisations in Scandic's practices complicated matters. The commercial availability of technological solutions was a problem. Obtaining funding support proved to be a challenge.

Processes applied

A common belief amongst management and team members that environmental responsibility was right was encouraged. Scandic's compass model was used to implement core values. Resource consumption was monitored, and waste reduced. Products with a lower environmental impact were purchased. Through publication, Scandic obtained external accreditation and recognition.

Networks utilised

Team members, local universities, consultants, peer organisation (Hilton Hotels), suppliers, accreditation bodies, media and customers.

Possible dilemmas

How can the company continue the project's momentum, within the various Scandic networks, in support of environmental responsibility? Will Scandic's quest for leadership recognition result in tangible benefits? How will financial returns be retained as start-up competitors take advantage of Scandic's environmental experience and build new operations without the cost of maintaining or replacing outdated resources? What will have to be done to maintain Scandic's brand superiority? Can new network formations help to mitigate some of these challenges?

Ecocean, Western Australia

Context

Ecocean is a small, not-for-profit marine conservation organisation researching the whale shark.

Declared innovation

The collaboration with NASA scientists as well as tourists in the generation of Ecocean scientific data that globally identified and tracked whale sharks.

Influence on sustainability

The dissemination of research findings describing the whale shark situation is expected to provide changes in human practice that will enhance sharks' sustainability. The developed systems could be useful in researching other threatened species.

Implementation drivers

As habitat was threatened and the apparent numbers of whale sharks decreased, tracking the movements of individual sharks was expected to lead to a better understanding of their ecology.

Barriers to achievement

Data collection had to be non-invasive. The number of global sightings needed to be increased. A method of identification was required. There was limited funding to support the research.

Processes applied

An internet presence was developed to promote awareness of the whale shark's plight and also as a system to disseminate photographs through user generated content.

Networks utilised

Peer researchers, research funding agencies, the media and tourists concerned about the wellbeing of whale sharks.

Possible dilemmas

How will Ecocean attract continuing financial support? What will happen if tourists cannot be relied upon to collect photographs? Is using amateurs, swimming with whale sharks, the most appropriate way to collect data and what is the possible bias involved? How can scientific research and tourist activities be combined in a manner that minimises the human impact on natural habitats? How can social networks or the rise of professional amateurs (Leadbeater & Miller 2004) help promote innovation and/or mitigate some of these challenges?

Xanterra LLC, Denver, Colorado, United States

Context

Xanterra is a highly complex organisation (the US's largest national park concessionaire, operating hotels, lodges, restaurants, retail, campgrounds and transportation systems in more than 20 locations), with 8,000 employees, numerous buildings (in Yellowstone National Park alone they have over 900 buildings) and third-party certification/audits, and is a corporation with shareholder responsibilities.

Declared innovation

The Environmental Management System (EMS) Ecologix provides a range of innovations (i.e. continual improvement of environmental performance, compliance with environmental regulations, best management practices and flexibility). Ecologix is described as a hybrid EMS because it includes aspects of compliance, sustainability and accountability.

Influence on sustainability

The overall benefits of Ecologix flow not only to the environment but also to the business performance of Xanterra. Increased environmental compliance, corrective action and monitoring of certification enabled Xanterra to provide leadership in environmentally focused tourism in a transformation toward more sustainable practices.

Implementation drivers

Xanterra's mission provides significant motivation amongst staff and this enthusiasm has been translated into the 2015 objectives. Also, environmental responsibility is considered to be 'the right thing to do'.

Barriers to achievement

Ecologix was an extensive and costly exercise. It remains to be seen whether the process translates into improved environmental performance; therefore, it was risky. The effectiveness of standards implementation depended upon the will and intention of the organisation. For Xanterra, top management support was critical, but there was also public and private agency interest in what happened in national parks. In the US, there is strong competition for park concessions; therefore, Xanterra has to be cost competitive and must also demonstrate strong environmental performance.

Processes applied

Employees were expected to hold management accountable by adopting a top-down mission and a bottom-up monitoring mechanism. The Ecologix EMS model was designed to achieve continuous improvement. Xanterra has a management structure that incorporates (environmental) objectives and targets into programs and procedures.

Networks utilised

Xanterra recruited the involvement of suppliers in the quest for environmental responsibility. Xanterra extended this responsibility to cuisine availability and accommodation practice and design.

Possible dilemmas

How should Xanterra ensure it achieves the 2015 objectives? What sustainability initiatives should Xanterra consider to underpin the successful management of competitive and cost pressures? How can Xanterra communicate environmental improvement so that shareholders and customers perceive a direct link to their wellbeing? How should the EMS evolve to provide sustainable competitive advantage? What will be the response of Xanterra's competitors to the Ecologix project?

Tasting Arizona, United States

Context

Tasting Arizona is a consortium of tourism, non-government, indigenous, farming, education, community, festival and food organisations.

Declared innovation

The decline in small US communities is being tackled by reviving community collaboration to produce local products and to stimulate traditional farming activities.

Influence on sustainability

The consortium aims to preserve traditional farming practices, conserve wildlife, educate youth, keep food free from genetic modification, maintain agricultural diversity and biodiversity, as well as protect cultural traditions.

Implementation drivers

There was a need to reinvigorate local habitat and conserve species that were under threat from human activity, as well as to retain the indigenous knowledge, cultural practices and values associated with this environment. However, stimulating local development by effectively utilising the natural environment was a major incentive.

Barriers to achievement

Large producer expectations impacted natural and farm land usage. Consumer choices needed to be changed in favour of local products. Small operators had difficulty achieving economies of scale and continuity of supply. Organic methods did not have the disease protection offered by the use of modern chemicals. There was competitive demand for water.

Processes applied

Community-supported agriculture attracted over 290 participants. Awareness was built amongst Arizona's youth. Local operators were enabled to get tourists to discover Arizona's produce and services.

Networks utilised

Local universities, non-profit federal and community groups, for-profit tourism operators, farmers and restaurants were included.

Possible dilemmas

To improve viability, should 'Tasting Arizona' consider how local products and services could be distributed outside Arizona? How can the formation of new networks or involvement with kindred networks (e.g. the Slow Food movement in Europe) help underpin sustainable innovation processes in the future? How can consumers be encouraged to select local products in preference to economic alternatives from other places? How can the competing community interests be managed in the long term? Can environmental and cultural benefits be described in specific economic terms? How will the appeal of a 'back to nature' lifestyle be sustained against the convenience of city life?

The Diablo Trust, Northern Arizona, USA

Context

The Diablo Trust was initiated in 1993 by two Arizona ranch families on the Bar T Bar and the Flying M Ranches. Membership of the Trust is diverse and includes ranchers, environmentalists, land managers, scientists and researchers.

Declared innovation

Communication amongst trust members is used to promote the social, biological and economic sustainability of federal, state and private lands; harmony between the natural environment and broader community is strived for by engaging in collaborative stewardship.

Influence on sustainability

The trust is seeking to maintain unfragmented landscapes and restore native ecosystems by promoting the long-term continuation of traditional working ranches (i.e. as economically viable enterprises).

Implementation drivers

There was a need to create a range of economic opportunities in support of private landholders and traditional users, whilst preserving open spaces for future generations. It was feared that traditional cattle ranches would not survive. Also, grasslands needed to be preserved not only for cattle but wildlife.

Barriers to achievement

Global trends in beef farming appeared to be contrary to cattle ranchers using ranges. Financial constraints associated with marketing 'trust' beef were a problem. Small-scale tourist activities were perceived to be economically difficult from both a human-resource and legal liability point of view. Finding new ways to use land that were aesthetically pleasing and did not dilute land holdings was challenging.

Processes applied

Formation of the trust as a regional planning area covering 426,000 acres enabled the land use plan to be developed. The trust undertook projects designed to enhance collaboration and learning about the land and the effects of management, recreation, climate, fire and time. Educational programs for local schools, wildlife protection, ranch management, community outreach and watershed improvements have been conducted.

Networks utilised

Land owners, local enterprises, government agencies and various community representatives.

Possible dilemmas

How can the trust ensure that member interests do not override the need to address common problems and thereby jeopardise future sustainability? What should be done to ensure that different levels of stakeholders' economic strength and political power be effectively harnessed for the common good? How can mutual trust encourage stakeholders to assign enforceable land use controls to the trust for the benefits of the community? How broadly should the 'common good' be defined? How can quality of life be promoted to attract visitors as well as future residents?

EDDA, Denmark

Context

To capitalise on the trend towards user-oriented and experience-driven economies (that embrace 'soft' aspects like identity, feelings, values, meanings, and aesthetics) a four-year project entitled 'Experience Development of Danish Attractions' (EDDA) was created. EDDA consists of 38 built attractions of varying size, theme and ownership structure that joined forces to share competence development and stimulate innovation.

Declared innovation

EDDA innovated by involving members in the development of competences, products, commodities and services; and this innovation extends from service and product development to management.

Influence on sustainability

EDDA aimed to support the sustainable development of member attractions as strong and innovative businesses by creating opportunities for competence development and experience exchange.

Implementation drivers

There was limited growth potential within the Danish attraction market. Competition was fierce within the attractions industry (and with other types of experience providers e.g. theatres, cinemas, game manufacturers, retailers). Expectations were not well categorised for the 'experience consumer'.

Barriers to achievement

There was a shortage of financial and human resources within participating EDDA attractions. In addition, there was initial reluctance and scepticism amongst employees and managers (this caused one attraction to leave EDDA). A lack of active contribution and commitment was expected. Trainers would need to adapt their course content to reflect the special needs of built attractions. The project would involve participants from all over Denmark and this constituted an organisational obstacle.

Processes applied

The project was guided by the principles of 'socially inclusive wealth creation' as a way to enhance the quality of life for all. A learning programme was developed that incorporated knowledge and tools, the latest learning methods, experiential discussion groups, implementation support and new network formation.

Networks utilised

All personnel from participating attractions were included. The leading organisation behind EDDA was the Development Fund for Tourist Attractions. EDDA included representatives from public and private tourism development and marketing entities. External networks of academics and practitioners were involved in knowledge dissemination and EDDA activities.

Possible dilemmas

What steps should EDDA take to secure ongoing financial support? Should EDDA continue to focus on learning as its key service? Should EDDA convert itself into a 'professional industry body' lobbying for members and providing member services? How can professional networks help to sustain learning and innovative behavior over time?

Brenu Beach Resort, Ghana

Context

A change of Ghanaian government had democratically taken place with a promise to invest in the local economy. There was wide-ranging goodwill and expectations of personal and professional freedom. The tourism industry was encouraged to invest in innovative business ideas. Small enterprises were seen as a way to improve the quality of life.

Declared innovation

In Ghana, the term innovation can be perceived as 'coping' or a constant survival process. Therefore, innovation is practiced to survive. This case describes a process of 'creating something meaningful out of nothing for a specific purpose or aim, using available and appropriate resources'.

Influence on sustainability

Auntie Aggie's ecotourism venture established an open air, do-it-yourself chop bar and restaurant. Typical Ghanaian dishes are cooked and generally eaten with the hands. Tourists are encouraged to contribute by cooking and by setting up a camp on the beach. Therefore, the venture sought to sustain a cultural lifestyle and to increase awareness of that culture.

Implementation drivers

The beach resort emanated from the owner's survival instincts and a need to develop a business using very limited resources.

Barriers to achievement

All of the essential means and structures needed to develop a small resort had to be developed. Auntie Aggie started with basic cooking utensils (such as charcoal pots) and three traditional cooking stones on a beach that traditionally belonged to her family. She struggled against social barriers and had minimal access to technological support. Land ownership/property rights were not well defined and misbehaviour was not necessarily dealt with fairly and justly.

Processes applied

Aunt Aggie' used a very simple process: determination to survive and willingness to develop a new business. She also relied on knowledge from customers of cultural backgrounds that were vastly different to her own.

Networks utilised

Tourists were a major source of ideas and support. They provided suggestions on how to run the business effectively as well as what to change or innovate. Local networks had to be established.

Possible dilemmas

How should Auntie Aggie handle new competitors as local people learn from her experience? What should Auntie Aggie do to ensure the co-operation of local community members, and could this help sustain traditional ways of life? Should Auntie Aggie embrace technology, including social media, to improve customer communications, loyalty and user-driven innovation, or strive to retain the authentic, rather 'unspoilt' ecotourism flavour of the resort? What safeguards should Auntie Aggie consider to ensure that powerful entrepreneurs do not over-whelm her venture?

AGSEP, Sri Lanka

Context

AGSEP is an NGO that has been conducting sport events and international exchanges between Sri Lankan and European sport teams. Based in Marawila, it was founded by its CEO (Dr Dietmar Döring) who was the national table tennis coach.

Declared innovation

AGSEP promotes 'active tourism' that has a socio-cultural focus. It combines travel with contribution to intercultural understanding and peace.

Influence on sustainability

By providing a positive socio-cultural experience that advanced the development of athletes and coaches, AGSEP promotes peace and well-being in Sri Lanka.

Implementation drivers

Relationships amongst Sri Lankan people were deeply divided. An activity that provided a neutral, peaceful and fun-bringing platform was needed. Sporting interaction was perceived to create collective feelings of passion, unity and a sense of community. There was a need to enhance local health and fitness, as well as to encourage understanding and learning. The economic development of the local community was in need of stimulation.

Barriers to achievement

The socio-political circumstances led to varying levels of safety and security concerns in Sri Lanka. The different values, customs and lifestyles of local residents (when compared to European tourists and international sport participants) were a challenge. Language differences were also a challenge.

Processes applied

The philosophy adopted was that sport is an ideal way of connecting people and transcending social, cultural, ethnic and religious divides. Exchange programmes that focused on sport development and individual training was the key process used. Selected Sri Lankans were invited to train with European experts. Furthermore, Sri Lankan sport coaches, trainers and support staff were invited to attend workshops, seminars and conferences.

Networks utilised

Local and international networks were used to achieve AGSEP objectives. Personal networks established initial co-operation. Local community support enabled access to an authentic Sri Lankan experience.

Possible dilemmas

How should the resort prepare for the intermittent disruptions caused by local unrest? What cultural values should the resort use to underwrite its activities (Sri Lankan or European)? How can the diversity of values be harnessed to inform future innovation processes? What level of corporate responsibility should AGSEP accept to ensure that local business and community interests benefit economically from arranged activities? Can a sustainable supplier strategy help drive innovation? What steps should AGSEP take to ensure long-term viability in the event of senior management change?

Integrating Tourism Communities: The Sustainable Tourism Laboratory, Blackstone Valley, Rhode Island, USA

Context

The Sustainable Tourism Laboratory (STL) assisted the Blackstone Valley Tourism Council (BVTC) to create a way in which to contribute to regional tourism development. STL's purpose is to promote the concept of planned sustainable tourism to local, regional, state, provincial and worldwide tourism leaders and community stakeholders.

Declared innovation

The STL is the key innovation. The laboratory is a community-based teaching and learning network that aims to advance sustainable tourism strategies.

Influence on sustainability

The concept of place-making focuses on an integrated holistic social, economic, ecological and cultural approach to community development. The BVTC environments are perceived to be elements of a large, whole system, or 'system of systems', that are interdependent and synergistic. STL adapts tourism processes in ways that support community values and enhances environmental sustainability.

Implementation drivers

Communities recognised the need to closely watch the immediate and emergent conditions within their environment. Effectively adapting to changing conditions was considered to be a pressing and urgent need. Ignoring the natural cycle of change would result in greater risk to communities.

Barriers to achievement

Planning between local, regional and global influences was complex and ineffective. Changing established procedure was resisted because previous processes had provided rewards. Creating a whole-place view, an intimate understanding of conditions and a strategic use of the adaptive cycle are all initial barriers to resilient innovation. Differing views of municipalities, organisations and innovators had to be overcome in order to adopt a resilient community perspective.

Processes applied

The STL is used as a community-based teaching and learning network. STL applies complex adaptive systems methods and thinking to community planning. Diverse elements like social, ecological, economic, education, cultural and built environments are understood to be interdependent.

Networks utilised

Starting in BVTC, the STL is considered to be a network that will expand the practice of resilience into tourism communities across the US and, eventually, the world. STL expects that as this network grows it will inspire interaction with other communities, leading to a global network of tourism professionals and practitioners.

Possible dilemmas

Should STL ground itself within the tourism arena or should it step up to embrace all forms of human planning? How should STL deal with community activities that are unsustainable? How can STL balance loyalties to influential individuals as well as local, regional, national or global interests? How can the STL use kindred international networks to advance future innovation processes?

Wenhai Ecolodge, Northwest Yunnan, China

Context

The Wenhai Ecolodge is situated in Northwest Yunnan, China. The Yunnan Province is ethnically, geographically and biologically diverse. The Ecolodge is a community-operated retreat run by a co-operative of 56 households with support from the US-based Nature Conservancy.

Declared innovation

The Ecolodge was created to provide an economical alternative to destructive practices such as illegal game hunting and poaching, logging and over-fishing. Members are encouraging the local community to use renewable energy to reduce tourism's drain on natural resources.

Influence on sustainability

Visitors to the Ecolodge generate interest in, and enthusiasm for, local culture and heritage. Therefore, the local community has a greater appreciation of its cultural heritage. Also, family traditions are being sustained by tourist interest.

Implementation drivers

There was a need to develop local economic activities. Natural resources were threatened and there was a need to demonstrate that sustainable tourism could be locally managed.

Barriers to achievement

There were local misconceptions about the tourism industry. Early tourist ventures produced unacceptable levels of pollution and environmental degradation. The finite nature of tourism resources was not appreciated. There was investment in tourism without consideration for sustainable planning and development. Therefore, previous tourist development made establishing the Ecolodge challenging.

Processes applied

The Ecolodge was required to donate at minimum 10 percent of net profits to conservation and community development. Visitor management systems are being established. Community members participated in the identification of the cultural traditions they wish to preserve. The impact of tourism is monitored to determine that Ecolodge supports the sustainability of local cultures.

Networks utilised

Northwest Yunnan Ecotourism Association was used and sponsored by the US-based Nature Conservancy and the Ecotourism Association was created to inform tourists about the unique ecotourism opportunities around Lijiang. The Ecolodge worked closely with local communities.

Possible dilemmas

What initiatives should Ecolodge consider to maintain its present state as the local community starts to push for modern improvements to their lifestyle? How should Ecolodge describe and communicate the benefits that result from protecting culture and heritage? Can the 'local culture' change in the process? If so, who will be the judge of how much, and which types of change are acceptable? How should Ecolodge ensure that the ecological and economic impacts of its activities are balanced? How should Ecolodge communicate its achievements to key stakeholders in ways that will encourage continued support? How can local participation help facilitate sustainable tourism?

Further issues arising from the case notes

Do these cases suggest contextual similarities? If so, would categorisation be useful? For example, can cases that describe small-scale, green initiatives be compared with cases situated within complex multi-organisational developments?

How do the cases provide insight into the conceptual use of innovation and sustainability when associated with tourism? For example, has innovation been depicted as radical change or small incremental improvements? Could the innovations be described as improvements in communication or in network resilience?

Have the cases adequately represented the holistic understanding of sustainability (social, cultural, environmental and economic aspects)? Are they biased toward the survival of individual or stakeholder interests? Should environmental factors take precedence in sustainable tourism? Is the incorporation of sustainability simply a convenient market-differentiating tool? How can the more intangible elements of cultural sustainability be described, and is there a need for tangible measurement (i.e. if it is not measured it does not count)?

How can tourism, innovation and sustainability issues be informed by the dilemmas that practitioners have to resolve? How can sustainable tourism help promote quality of life, for tourists and residents alike? Will technology, and especially new social media, change how networks for sustainable tourism operate?

References

Leadbeater, C & Miller, P 2004, *The Pro-Am Revolution. How enthusiasts are changing our economy and society*, accessed 4 April 2012, www.demos.co.uk/files/proamrevolutionfinal.pdf?1240939425.

Index